T0160310

A **DUARTE** GUIDE

Presenting Virtually

Table of Contents

Foreword   VI

Introduction
Connect From a Distance   1

Context
Understand the Virtual Medium   9
Analyze the Challenges   14
Explore the Benefits   19
Embrace the New Golden Rule   25

Strategy
Plan Your Presentation   35
Empathize With Your Audience   38
Choose Your Format   44
Communicate in Multiple Dimensions   51

Story
Craft Content That Holds Attention   59
Make Your Content Consumable   62
Fine-Tune Your Structure   71
Manage Their Distractibility   80
Orchestrate Purposeful Interactions   84

A **DUARTE** GUIDE

Presenting Virtually

Communicate
and Connect With
Online Audiences

PATTI SANCHEZ

Mountain View,
California

DUARTE
PRESS

Published in the United States of America by Duarte Press, LLC.
www.duarte.com

All trademarks are the property of their respective companies.

Design by Duarte, Inc.

Cataloging in publication data is on file with the Library of Congress.
ISBN 978-1-64687-073-8

Special Sales
Duarte Press, LLC books are available at a special discount for bulk
purchases for corporate training programs or sales promotions.
For more details, email contact@duarte.com.

Visuals

Design for All Dimensions 93
Curate Your Backdrop 96
Design Your Graphics 103
Plan Your Presence 116

Delivery

Command the Virtual Room 125
Step Up Your Setup 128
Optimize Your Tech 133
Make the Most of Your Voice 146
Move With Intention 153

Conclusion

Make a World of Difference 163

Appendix

Virtual Presentation Checklist 168
Glossary 173
References 179
Photo Credits 189
Acknowledgements 191
Index 193
About the Author 199

Foreword

Virtual presenting is not new, but it's newly common. Almost overnight in 2020, much of the world dispersed into work-from-home environments. In some ways, we lost touch; in others, we became closer. Suddenly, we could peer into the living rooms of CEOs and watch a co-worker's cat saunter across their desk.

Spending over a year working remotely has altered how people communicate. Professional public speakers are opting to deliver virtual-only presentations, often for the same fees as in-person. Global sales teams are gaining efficiencies by pitching virtually instead of flying to Tokyo or Las Vegas for a one-hour meeting. Executives who delighted audiences in person now have to woo cameras, with no real-time feedback on how their message is resonating. Speakers of all kinds are still figuring out how to make eye contact and keep people engaged from the other side of a screen. Love it or hate it, virtual presenting is here for the long haul. You need to be good at it.

The insights in this guidebook are based on real-world expertise. They're drawn from our collective experience at Duarte, where the author, Patti Sanchez, has been a senior executive since 2011. As a company, we've creatively and rapidly transformed some of the world's largest gatherings for the most admired brands into virtual events. Patti brought her strategy and storytelling smarts to those efforts. Plus, her team reconstructed our communication workshops as remote offerings—and they did so in such a clever, interactive, and engaging way that our virtual courses receive the highest ratings and are selling out. Patti has synthesized what we've learned solving problems for our clients and for ourselves into practical tips that people at any organization, at any level, can use.

Our hope is that this guide helps you communicate your best from anywhere.

Nancy

Nancy Duarte
CEO and Author

Introduction
Connect From a Distance

As organizations increasingly operate in a virtual or hybrid fashion, the ability to communicate well online is becoming an indispensable skill. New job opportunities and increased responsibility will flow to those who know how to give effective and appealing virtual presentations.

If you're like most knowledge workers, including me, you're doing your job remotely some or all of the time or working with remote colleagues. While telecommuting has existed for decades, it wasn't considered the norm until 2020, when the COVID-19 pandemic forced companies around the world to rapidly change how they operated.

Despite the stress of managing in a crisis, businesses that previously resisted telework discovered they could get things done efficiently and effectively when people weren't tethered to their offices or tied up by travel.[1] Beyond productivity gains, organizations that pivoted their operations and events from physical to virtual saw reductions in expenses as well as carbon emissions.[2] Thanks to these economic benefits of remote work, what started as a temporary measure is becoming a way of life. And I think, on balance, we're better off for it.

The future is virtual

The research firm Gartner projects that 74% of companies will adopt remote work permanently for some employees[3] and that by 2024 only 25% of business meetings will happen in person.[4] We can expect similar trends for conferences and other events. Even businesses that resume in-person gatherings plan to incorporate online components, which means that hybrid meetings and events—blending virtual and physical—are gaining momentum.[5]

So it's no surprise that virtual communication technologies are being widely adopted. Pew Research Center found that 81% of people who work from home use video conferencing and the majority of teleworkers (65%) think a combination of video and instant messaging is a suitable alternative to in-person communication.[6] However, many people who were teleworking for the first time in 2020 said they felt less connected when collaborating remotely. That's a critical challenge in this new world of work. We must all learn how to connect with others from a distance.

You have the tools

Remote communication can mean anything from responding to an instant message from your boss to crafting an email to a customer to running a team meeting online. But this book will focus on virtual presentations—situations where you are speaking to a group of people who aren't in the room with you, using visual, verbal, and nonverbal techniques to get them to adopt your ideas. These talks can be formal or informal. In most cases, they are delivered through web-based collaboration apps or videoconferencing platforms—digital tools that many businesses already have in place and that many people know how to use, at least at a beginner's level.

Creating and delivering an in-person presentation usually involves sharing information on slides, using software like PowerPoint®, Keynote®, Prezi® or Google Slides™. Some presenters go the analog route, writing on whiteboards and sticky notes. You can still use all of those tools when presenting remotely—by sharing slides or whiteboards on a virtual platform, for instance, or even holding handwritten notes up to your camera. But virtual platforms provide other options, as well, such as using a photo or graphic as your backdrop, annotating on top of slides, and facilitating dialogue via chat windows or in digital breakout rooms.

Really, anything that is seen or heard by the audience online is part of the show. That includes the very basics of communication: your words, vocal inflections, facial expressions, and physical gestures. You have all that in your digital toolkit, too.

Now you need the skills

Through virtual presentations, you can address audiences in multiple locations at the same time, vastly expanding the reach of your ideas—if your presentation can hold their interest well enough to get your message across.

While delivering a presentation online gives you powerful capabilities, it also creates complexity that can send speakers into a tailspin. We've all seen people stumble with the technology—struggling to unmute themselves after being introduced, accidentally showing the wrong file when trying to bring up their slides, totally missing chats from attendees because too many windows were open on the presenter's screen. But even moderately tech-savvy speakers grapple with challenges like getting their lighting right, minimizing background noise, and remembering to look into the camera instead of at their slides. Then there are presenters who feed off the energy of a live audience but tend to fizzle out when addressing a camera that doesn't smile or laugh at their jokes.

If not managed with care, all these factors can create barriers between you and your virtual audience. Their attention will quickly wander toward something less taxing and more compelling—perhaps an email that just landed in their inbox, a news alert that popped up on their phone, or the view through their home office window.

Success starts here

Given those potential barriers, your virtual presentation needs to be as good, if not better, than what you would deliver in person. If that sounds like a daunting task, don't worry. You can do this, and I'm here to help you make it happen. In the pages that follow, you'll find the techniques and tips you'll need, including how to:

- Choose the right type of virtual presentation to reach your audience in a given situation

- Use communication technology to strengthen connections so you and your ideas will shine, even from a distance

- Plan and write presentation content that will keep your remote audience engrossed

- Create visuals that make you and your content stand out online

- Polish your delivery so you can build rapport through the camera

Before delving into those concrete tips, I'll lay some conceptual groundwork, exploring challenges you'll face and opportunities you can seize as a virtual presenter.

Let's get started.

01

Context
Understand the Virtual Medium

Virtual communication empowers people to express ideas in new ways. Yet if it's not used well, the medium can leave audiences cold. By exploiting its benefits and minimizing its drawbacks, remote presenters can create experiences that delight and move audiences.

Adopting digital tools for communication makes our lives easier in some respects, harder in others. For instance, when many companies rapidly pivoted to remote work in 2020, they turned to virtual meeting platforms to keep projects and teams on track. But those same tools soon became a source of frustration for people who found themselves locked in virtual meetings for hours on end. "Zoom fatigue" became a hot topic for a reason.[7]

When people hear that phrase, it resonates. It succinctly captures their pain. But it also paints a simplistic, one-dimensional picture of a medium that's rich and multifaceted. To master any medium, users must understand the challenges it creates as well as the potential it holds.

In his classic work, *Laws of Media*,[8] media theorist Marshall McLuhan argued that each time a new medium appears, it brings with it four effects, all at once. The new medium:

- Enhances communication
- Retrieves some aspects of earlier media
- Obsolesces, or displaces, other forms of media
- Reverses, or overturns, its original benefits if overused

Nancy Duarte wrote in her *HBR Guide to Persuasive Presentations*[9] that these laws of media can be applied to remote presentations, but since then new challenges and opportunities have emerged as virtual presenting has grown and evolved *(Figure 1)*.

FIGURE 1

McLuhan's Laws Applied to Virtual Presentations

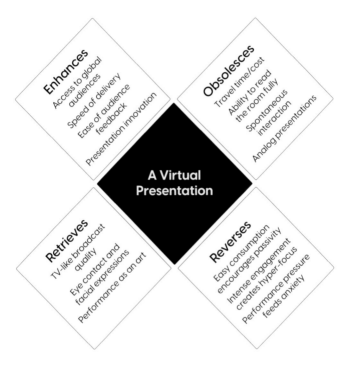

Because technology erects a barrier between speakers and audiences, a virtual talk is a step removed from a physical one. That distance has its drawbacks: It can dilute the speaker's impact, make the audience feel isolated, and allow myriad distractions (some of them technological) to creep in and compete for attention. Yet, the same technology also brings several benefits. For instance, speakers can reach broader audiences and connect more intimately with large groups than they would in person. Digital tools also give speakers new ways to creatively express their ideas and transform how they communicate.

This section will explore these pros and cons so you can manage both effectively later on, when you're planning, creating, and delivering your virtual presentation.

Analyze the Challenges

Virtual presentations change how you come across to audiences. Even the very best presenters you know—the CEO who holds employees in thrall whenever they speak, the charismatic entrepreneur who nails every pitch, the TED speaker whose talk you've watched a dozen times—are reduced to smaller, flatter versions of themselves when viewed online. The same is true for you, too. It's not your fault; blame the technology and devices that stand between you and your audience. You can counter those effects, though, with quality, novelty and interaction.

Overcome dilution with high quality

When you give a virtual presentation, technology acts as an intermediary between you and your audience *(Figure 2)*. Your laptop and other equipment convert and compress your audio and video into digital bits that will travel quickly through the web and reach your viewers intact. But that trip through cyberspace can dilute your impact by making your image and voice less vivid than you are in real life. An occasional internet hiccup on either end can cause video to freeze or audio to become garbled, making it harder for your message to come across clearly. Also, the audience may have minimized the window in which they view your presentation, further diminishing your presence.

FIGURE 2

Technology Adds Layers Between You and Your Audience

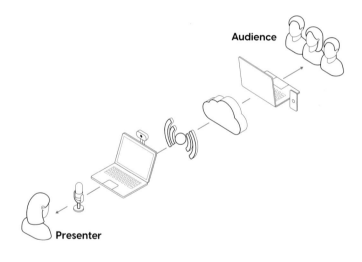

Though audiences have come to expect these tradeoffs as part of digital life, you can make the loss of richness less problematic by putting out a higher-quality product from the start. Making some basic upgrades—for instance, investing in the highest-speed internet available, a fast computer with extra processing power, and a professional microphone and camera—can take your presentation up a notch so you'll lose less in translation.

Combat distraction with novelty

If you put in extra effort to overcome technical constraints and provide your audience with a better experience, what they see and hear will be higher quality than the average virtual presentation—if they're paying attention. But audiences who watch presentations online, whether at work or at home, are significantly more likely to be distracted than "captive" in-person audiences. In a 2020 study by HR services firm JDP, 54% of over 2,000 Americans who had recently switched to remote work said they were more distracted at home, and 29% said they were more distracted at the office.[10] At the office, your audience could be interrupted by any number of things: incoming emails from customers, instant messages from co-workers, a phone call from the boss, text messages from a spouse, even a simple reminder that they've got something due by the end of the day. At home, they're vulnerable to those same types of distractions, plus others: barking dogs inside, leaf blowers outside, the doorbell, or the kiddo who really, really, really needs help right now.

When an interruption occurs, you've lost your audience's focus, and it's up to you to win it back. To do that, use novelty as a device to regain people's attention. Our brains are always on the alert for changes in our environment.[11] So, if you inject some element of change into your virtual presentation— include an image in your slides that's unlike the others, alter your tone of voice, invite people to interact with you in a new way—your audience will be compelled to look again and listen more closely. Novel stimuli and experiences flood the brain with dopamine, the chemical associated with rewards, like good food, good music, and good times. Dopamine makes us happier and, as neuroscientists have discovered, accelerates learning.[12] By crafting a presentation that surprises and delights using the tips in later sections of this book, you'll see higher audience engagement.

Ward off isolation with interaction

Humans are inherently social animals, but many aren't getting the bonding and interaction they crave. In a survey of more than 10,000 U.S. workers, conducted in 2019, three out of five reported feeling lonely.[13] So this isn't a new problem, but the major shift to remote work raises the risks.[14] What's more, feelings of isolation and loneliness tend to increase anxiety and depression, which are at an all-time high worldwide.[15]

All of this means that a large percentage of your online audience probably needs a boost of human connection. If you avoid looking into the camera or give one-way lectures, people will only feel further alienated.

Instead, make your audience feel included by involving them. In research conducted by Duarte, the majority of respondents said they prefer live virtual presentations to recorded ones and appreciate having a variety of ways to engage and interact with speakers and peers.[16] Virtual communication platforms provide a host of interactive features, including chat, Q&A, polls, and breakout rooms, all of which you can use to bridge the gap between you and your audience. We'll discuss how to craft interaction strategies in the Story section beginning on page 59.

Explore the Benefits

When a new technology is announced, its evangelists paint a picture of the bright future it will usher in for its users. They promise we'll be better off because the fancy new gadget we just bought will let us do things we'd never dreamed were possible before. Sure, it's hype, but there's often some truth to it. That's certainly the case with virtual meeting and collaboration platforms, which have led to new ways of interacting and expressing ideas. Communicating will never be the same as it used to be, and that can be a good thing.

Reach anyone, anywhere

Of all the benefits virtual presentations afford, increased reach is the greatest reward according to communicators surveyed by Duarte.[17] Remote communication removes barriers to growth by making geographical distance practically irrelevant. With a virtual foundation, businesses can serve customers and recruit diverse talent in other regions. Freed from the constraints of travel, sales reps and clients can interact more often. So can employees, who don't have to hop in a car or on a plane to meet with managers and colleagues in other locations. As a speaker, you, too, have more freedom and greater access to people than before.

When you remove the requirements to travel to a physical venue, you open up a whole new world of presenting possibilities—literally. If you're located in the U.S., for example, you could get up early to deliver a presentation to customers in Europe, update your local team midmorning on how the idea was received, and spend your afternoon planting that seed with business partners in Southeast Asia and seeking their input. Because you can reach anyone who has an internet connection, your ideas can travel around the globe in a single day. Even if you're communicating with people in your own time zone, they're more likely to join on a tightly scheduled day if they can easily tune in between other meetings, without having to sprint from place to place.

To realize these advantages, think about opening up your talks to audiences you might not normally address. For instance, perhaps you've only presented to local or national chapters of your favorite professional associations, but now you can reach the international chapters of those same groups. Or if your company hosts live webinars or workshops, consider hosting multiple sessions in different time zones to accommodate viewers in far-off regions. Doing so will not only increase reach but also foster inclusion by enabling audiences who can't easily attend meetings or events in-person to access your content. Erasing such boundaries is beneficial for business and society, too.

Get closer than before

As a virtual presenter, you have an edge over speakers in giant auditoriums, lecture halls, or even large conference rooms. In those venues, which can be packed with people, slides are often projected onto a huge screen behind you, drawing your audience's eyes to your visuals while you compete for their attention. But in a virtual setting, you're in much closer proximity to your viewers—maybe a foot or two away. When looking into your camera while sitting at a laptop, you can gaze through the lens, into their eyes, as easily as a friend chatting over a cup of coffee.

Looking directly into the camera can be a challenge for presenters who are accustomed to speaking in person, just as moving from stage to television is a leap for many actors. But eye contact is essential to make your message feel direct and personal, which deepens your connection with your audience. TV show hosts have long embraced this dynamic to build relationships with viewers. Famous for his ability to bond with children, Fred Rogers used to picture a specific young audience in his mind while looking into the camera lens to tape *Mister Rogers' Neighborhood*. He said, "I think of the children I know and aspects of life they are dealing with. I don't think of a whole lot of people when I look at the television camera. It is a very, very personal medium."[18]

Comedian Stephen Colbert was surprised by how profoundly the casual format of the "at home" version of *The Late Show* affected his own delivery. Previously, Colbert recorded daily episodes in front of a live studio audience at Ed Sullivan Theater in New York, and like many comedians he fed off the crowd's reactions. While he lost that real-time feedback broadcasting from home, he discovered the new format brought him closer to his viewers in a different way. "That intimacy was something I didn't realize I missed, until I got it back," Colbert says. "It's less intimate to be in front of 450 people and the camera is 25 feet away from you, not four feet away."[19]

Virtual proximity makes your face clearly visible, too, so be mindful of what you're conveying there. Annoyance, impatience, and other negative feelings have a way of making themselves known if you're not careful. I speak from experience. Because my face is a mirror of my internal state, I've had to work on maintaining an expression during particularly challenging virtual meetings. I try to harness the positive, as well, remembering to smile more when I'm speaking online to make the affection I feel for my audience more visible to them. Through subtle facial expressions, you, too, can engage people with emotional nuances that would get lost at a greater distance. If you're excited to share a big idea or sad to bear disappointing news, they'll see it and feel it.

That closeness can also have a democratizing effect on the relationship between speaker and audience. Executives who once seemed aloof or stilted when presenting from a stage at an event become more accessible and relatable when they're joining a video meeting from a cluttered desk in their home office. An executive speaker coach, Jeff, puts it this way: "I'm a 6'1" guy, and I can be intimidating in person. But in a virtual meeting, you and I are the same size, and that changes the dynamic." Jeff goes on to say, "I also feel like I know a CEO better if I'm watching him or her on a screen in my living room." That's especially true if the CEO's kid barges in during the meeting or their dog goes ballistic when the doorbell rings. Being "seen" in a personal context levels the field and puts our humanity front and center, reminding us that we're more alike than different on the inside.

Deliver a cohesive experience

Besides bridging physical and emotional distances, virtual meeting and event platforms can help speakers create and deliver a different kind of presentation altogether. Initially, these platforms merely let speakers share slides in a separate window. This is a valid function, especially if your goal is to draw attention to the content of your deck by giving it a lot of screen space. But virtual platforms are quickly evolving to do more.

You can now integrate digital whiteboards and other applications, virtual backgrounds, videos, accessibility features, and even slides into one cohesive experience for the viewer. For instance, you can use a video as your background to add movement into your virtual environment. Or you can share an entire slide presentation as a backdrop, as if you were standing in front of your slides in a face-to-face presentation. This lets you use your hands to draw attention to the graphics that surround you. The main benefit of a visually integrated approach is that the audience doesn't have to work as hard to follow what you are saying while also digesting what you are showing because both streams of information co-exist harmoniously in a single frame.

And there's another upside, with some caveats: When visual elements are integrated into one environment, you can present ideas in front of things you can't stand in front of in real life. You can transport yourself to a different place, like another country (or planet), using virtual backgrounds. Some of us remote workers like to hide our messy home offices by personalizing our backgrounds with vacation photos or by cribbing images from our favorite home design blogs. But the novelty of fake virtual backgrounds is quickly wearing off, and now they are more likely to make people wonder, "What are you *really* hiding back there?" Your creativity should always serve your main purpose as a presenter: connecting with people and getting them to engage with your ideas. When you're ready to choose your graphics, do so with that highly practical goal in mind, following advice in the Visuals section of this book, beginning on page 93.

Embrace the New Golden Rule

Audiences expect more now from virtual presentations than they initially did. It's time, then, to put ourselves in their shoes so we can discover and deliver what they want. Duarte has long championed this golden rule: *Never deliver a presentation you wouldn't want to sit through*. That means putting the audience's needs and experience at the center of every choice you make as a presenter. But now that we've learned virtual presentations can be harder to sit through than in-person talks, given all the room for distraction, we're due for an update: *Never deliver a virtual presentation that is less engaging than it would have been in person*.

You can boost audience engagement by borrowing ideas and inspiration from other media. The term "virtual presentation" may conjure a high-tech concept in your mind, but it's just an extension of other forms of communication that came before it. And we can learn a lot about moving audiences from TV and radio.

Hold attention with dynamic audio

Radio is considered the first mass broadcast medium because it allowed communicators to spread their message widely over a large geographic area. While the underlying technology was originally used for one-to-one communication, radio is a one-to-many medium. When it emerged, communicators had to adapt so they could hold the attention of a group of listeners, rather than a single pair of ears.

Radio stations appealed to the interests of mixed audiences by varying program formats. Over the course of a day, a station schedule might include peaceful instrumental songs, readings from a poet or a preacher, a maudlin soap opera, talent shows or comedy acts, and thrilling mystery tales. Even within a single show, creators would use dynamic, contrasting sounds to make the air crackle with energy and keep listeners glued to their radios. Performers with wildly different voices crisply articulated their lines so the dialogue would be easier to follow in noisy parlors, bars, and cars. At times, their words were punctuated by vibrant music, clever sound effects, or dramatic pauses that left listeners wondering what could possibly happen next.[20]

Building dynamic audio into your virtual presentation— by varying the pitch, tone, volume, and pace of your own voice, and incorporating others' voices when appropriate —can mesmerize your audience, too.

Connect through cameras

Television built on the innovations of radio, enabling broadcasters to bring vivid sounds and visuals together. Audiences were awestruck by the combination. In 1937, TV maker R.C.A. demonstrated a version of the technology in front of 200 journalists gathered at its corporate headquarters in New York. One writer who was present that day, Jessie Wiley Voils, described what she experienced this way: "As we sat in the dark, there in the lid of the wonder machine appeared the small but clear image... David Sarnoff, president of R.C.A... bowed and smiled and started speaking... When the lights went on, I glanced down at my notebook. Only four words were written there: 'What next! What next!'"[21] That early "wonder machine" captured imaginations and transported us all into the future of communication.

But it took time for communicators to discover what they could do with that machine. At first, TV show creators and performers merely repeated techniques they'd used in radio or theater, but the overall effect was lackluster when viewed on a small screen. It wasn't until people tapped into the unique potential of cameras that the medium of TV came into its own. Artists from the Golden Age of TV like comedian Ernie Kovacs soon realized the camera was a tool they could use to connect with audiences and surprise them with unexpected intimacy. For instance, Kovacs would sometimes interrupt a comedy sketch to look straight into the camera and address the audience directly, or he'd have the camera follow him as he went backstage to his "real" office and invited viewers to come right in.[22]

Another early TV talent, Dave Garroway (who helped break ground with the talk show format), once said, "Television is an intrinsically personal medium simply because when you watch somebody perform in your living room you feel much closer."[23] Modern TV personalities and crews, like Jimmy Fallon and his production team, learned to leverage the intimacy and creativity that virtual communication allows to make their home-bound shows more vivid and interesting.[24] Virtual presentations, which bring speakers into the offices and homes of their viewers, can feel just as personal.

As seasoned TV performers do, use what viewers see through your camera to build rapport with them while you're there. Pay special attention to your facial expressions to convey the feelings you want to express, whether that's seriousness, excitement, surprise, or delight. Also consider how you can use your hands and physical gestures to underscore key points. We'll explore how to do that effectively later in the book, in the section on Delivery, beginning on page 125, so you can keep audiences captivated through the lens.

Find your inner pioneer

There are as many ways to make virtual presentations engaging as there are presenters in the world. You can learn a lot from media innovators of the past, as well as from contemporary presenters you admire. But ultimately, it's what you choose to do with what you learn that will help you connect with audiences in a distinctive, memorable way.

If you apply the principles in this book with a spirit of inventiveness, you can rise above the challenges of the medium and deliver virtual presentations that are far better than the others people have to attend all day long. You might even become a more compelling speaker when presenting online, as I have found.

Presenting has always been a key part of my job as a communication consultant, yet for years I still got butterflies every time I had to step on a stage. (At heart, I'm a bit of an introvert.) But the virtual medium has felt liberating, because the audience can see only part of me—what I choose to share on screen. That's made me a bolder speaker. And I'm having fun experimenting with virtual presentation tools that give me new options for sharing slides and interacting with audience members. As a result, I'm getting higher audience ratings than ever for my talks, and I'm sure you will, too, using the techniques in the sections that follow.

Case study
How tech leaders pivoted to virtual events

Events are a core communication channel for most companies, particularly for technology brands that rely on gatherings to convene customers, partners, and employees and drive conversation around the latest products being launched. Historically, tech conferences have been held in person at showy locations, with millions of dollars spent on renting and decorating massive spaces to create epic environments that wow onsite audiences. When the COVID-19 pandemic forced a pivot to virtual platforms, resourceful event organizers saw it as a springboard for innovation, leading many to make changes that may stick for a long time. Three tech companies in particular —Salesforce, Apple, Microsoft—forged new ground with inventive formats *(Figure 3)*.

Salesforce was set to begin its "World Tour" in Sydney, Australia, in early March 2020, when the pandemic put an end to travel. Rooms in a large conference center had long ago been booked and outfitted with elaborate sets designed in the company's distinctive look and feel. Instead of cancelling the event entirely and letting the pricey space sit empty, Salesforce event planners chose to convert it into a makeshift broadcast studio for livestreamed presentations. Speakers stood before the stunning backdrops to deliver their talks while multiple camera operators switched views between their faces and their slides, giving audiences a front-row seat at every session.

FIGURE 3

Examples of Virtual Presentations From Tech Leaders

Event stages were repurposed as studios for Salesforce's virtual world tour

A digital core powered Microsoft's flagship developer event, Build

TV-like graphics brought extra polish to Apple's digital developer conference

After the live sessions, online attendees could explore rooms in a virtual expo center to learn about featured products and pose questions to Salesforce experts and early-adopter customers, who the company calls "trailblazers."[25] Salesforce evolved the format further for the company's flagship event, Dreamforce. What used to be a four-day face-to-face event was transformed into a multi-week digital experience filled with live and on-demand presentations, training workshops, performances, and customer-specific sessions, all hosted within the company's web-based product.[26]

Another tech giant renowned for its in-person events, Apple had to reimagine its famous Worldwide Developer Conference (WWDC) as a digital experience in 2020. In prior years, the exclusive event typically filled multiple conference centers in San Francisco and San Jose before it was moved to the company's redesigned headquarters in Cupertino, California. But the virtual format gave the Apple event team an opportunity to reach a more global audience across 155 countries, unlocking an unprecedented level of accessibility that made their 2020 event the biggest WWDC gathering ever. Design has always been a differentiator for the Apple brand, so the visual quality of presentations couldn't be compromised, despite the lack of splashy giant screens to display the speakers' graphics. Instead, the event team opted to kick the impact of visuals up several levels by prerecording all sessions so sophisticated graphics could be intertwined with verbal narratives spoken by presenters. While opening remarks by

CEO Tim Cook were delivered from Steve Jobs Theater as in previous years, other sessions were recorded in locations around Apple Park. Speakers who were less experienced at playing to a camera lens were given extra delivery coaching to help them convey their key points while maintaining eye contact. The result? An event that some long-time WWDC attendees said was not only more accessible but also "more exciting than usual."[27]

Pushing the concept of an online event even further, Microsoft envisioned a wholly different kind of digital experience that would take full advantage of the medium. Rather than streaming a physical conference, the software maker chose to design its event around a "digital core," with all content and interactions streaming from the company's Teams collaboration application and Azure cloud computing platform. Borrowing a concept from software development known as "follow the sun"—where development happens around the clock—Microsoft's event organizers conceived the conference as a 24/7 television network that would broadcast content at all hours of the day and night, featuring a mix of live and pre-recorded sessions emceed by live "anchors." As soon as the team latched onto that television metaphor, it unleashed their creativity and inspired new thinking about everything from the flow of the overall event to length and format of individual sessions to the experience before, during, and after each session. Bob Bejan, Corporate Vice President and head of global events at Microsoft, put it this way: "Audiences aren't captivated by an hourlong stream of a single camera pointed at a person on a stage. Instead, plan that hour in segments. Use multiple cameras and frames to change angles. The presenter must tune their performance to the intimacy of the camera, like a movie or television performer. Remember, you are making television now."[28] Emboldened by the success of its digital strategy—which resulted in a 2500% increase in attendance, a 50% decrease in costs, and dramatic reductions in carbon emissions— Microsoft plans to make digital the bedrock of its events into the future.

Whether events are held virtually or in a hybrid setting that includes both live and remote audiences, it's clear that the nature of presentations has changed forever. Proficiency in this medium will give you an edge when it comes time to present online. But you might be surprised to learn how many of the techniques used by top brands are accessible and affordable to you. Read on to learn how to plan, write, design, and deliver virtual presentations that communicate and connect with remote audiences.

02

Strategy
Plan Your Presentation

Great communication starts with a strong foundation: a well-defined goal and a strategy to achieve it. For an online presentation, that means understanding your audience well enough to deliver information in the format that will successfully involve and influence them.

Any seasoned public speaker knows you've got to prepare before you present. At Duarte, our speechwriters won't start tapping out the first words of a script until they've considered the speaker's goals, explored the audience's needs, and defined the big idea that needs to be communicated. Similarly, our designers spend time thinking conceptually about style, format, and likely use cases before they even open up a slidemaking app. We've all learned that diligent groundwork makes for better presentations, and that same principle applies to your virtual talks.

As with in-person talks, you should carefully choose the format that will best equip you to persuade your particular audience. But speaking remotely adds another wrinkle to your planning: You'll also have to consider the various settings and situations people may be in when they're watching you. Sorting out all these variables will help determine how you'll want to interact with viewers, which will later influence your content, visuals, and delivery.

Before you can decide any of that, though, first identify your goals for the audience: how you want them to think and feel during your presentation and what you want them to do when it's over. If you put yourself in their shoes from the start, you can make focused choices in support of moving them to act. So we'll talk about how to empathize with your remote audience before we get into choosing the best format, tools, and more.

Empathize With Your Audience

When presenting, your role is to serve your audience. After all, they are the reason you are even giving a talk—and they are the ones who decide whether your ideas will go anywhere. They may choose to accept or reject your ideas, amplify or ridicule them, take action or not. That's why it makes sense to kick off your planning process by thinking about the world as your audience sees it.

Adopt their perspective

Begin by forming a mental image of your intended audience. To conjure up a clear picture, consider not only who these people are but also how they might receive or resist the messages you share with them. You can get into their heads by anticipating what they will think about your idea, how they will feel about it, and how they might behave as a result. In psychology, this is called perspective-taking,[29] because it involves assuming alternate points of view with the goal of understanding others better. It's the essence of empathy, and it's vital for persuasion.

Exploring your audience's mindset like this helps you determine what you can say and do to move people. Imagine what thoughts and feelings they are likely to have on the topic before you've spoken about it. Then think about how you would like to see their thoughts, feelings, and actions change after you're done speaking. These "before" and "after" states define the journey you will take with your audience—moving them from one place to another—to persuade them to adopt your idea. Finally, brainstorm how you will achieve this shift in your audience during your virtual presentation, being mindful of both the message you want to deliver and the medium you're using.

For example, let's assume you've been asked to give a presentation about the status of your team's projects at a virtual meeting of your company's leaders. Your explicit goal is to convince the executive team that your projects are all running smoothly and to highlight positive results for the business overall. But you also have a secret goal: to impress them with your leadership skills, because you're eager to take on a bigger role in the not-too-distant future and you'd like to position yourself accordingly. Shaping your audience's perception of you while also delivering the information they want to hear will require some planning and nuanced persuasion, especially for a busy executive audience. Plot out their potential thoughts, feelings, and actions to figure out how to move them *(Figure 4)*.

Given your audience's keen interest in how your projects are feeding the business and whether they're yielding the

FIGURE 4

Plotting the Audience's Journey: A Sample Presentation
to Executive Decision-Makers

Move From	Move To	By
Thoughts		
Wondering about status	Believing all is going well	Sharing project status
Questioning ROI	Seeing business results	Emphasizing impact
Feelings		
Curious, concerned	Confident, reassured	Speaking clearly Making eye contact
Actions		
Requesting more information	Increasing speaker's job responsibilities	Highlighting leadership principles used

expected return for all the money and time invested, that
context should shape your pitch. You'll want to reassure
company leaders on both fronts while making your way
onto their short-list of people to be considered for increased
responsibility. As you share project updates and results, shed
light on how you helped your team achieve those results.
Perhaps share a quick story about a challenging problem that
cropped up and describe how you addressed it as a leader
while also giving due credit to your team for their hard work

and accomplishments. After building a presentation that communicates your project's business value and reflects your thoughtful, supportive approach to team leadership, rehearse using your virtual setup to make sure you show up as confidently as possible by speaking clearly and maintaining eye contact with the camera. Thanks to this planning and preparation, you will create such a positive impression that the exec team will remember your words and your impact on the company after you leave the room.

Consider their viewing environment

Exploring the perspective of your audience will help you plan a virtual presentation that is relevant and persuasive. But you also need to take stock of the situation in which they are watching you speak, because it affects their ability to focus and participate effectively. In particular, think about when and where they'll be viewing your talk online and what else could be competing for their attention *(Figure 5)*.

Perhaps people will be watching your talk at the office, because you're presenting at a company meeting, for example, or they've signed up to attend your live webinar for professional development. If so, chances are pretty good that they'll watch on a decent-sized screen where your slides and video should be easy to see. But they may also feel pressure to get other things done at the same time, choosing to minimize the size of your video on their screen so they can keep email open in another window to respond to requests while you present.

FIGURE 5

What Audiences Might Be Doing While Viewing
Your Presentation

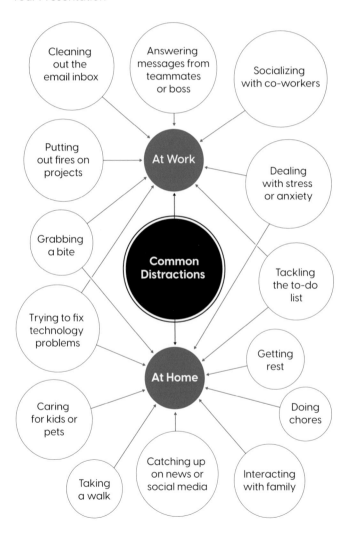

If people are watching your presentation at home, that increases the chances they'll be looking at it on a mobile device, which means your slides, video, and physical gestures and expressions will be smaller and harder to see. Plus, your presentation will be competing with personal demands, like getting in some exercise, taking care of someone else, or simply going to bed on time—in addition to any work tasks waiting to be done. Or your audience may want to consume your presentation while commuting or working out, when it's easier to listen than to watch.

Realize, too, that consuming information is easier for some people than others. Members of your online audience may have visual or auditory impairments or find it hard to process information at the speed you tend to deliver it. So as you take a walk in your audiences' shoes, consider ways to make your presentation as accessible as possible.[30] Be sure your virtual communication platform offers assistive technologies like closed-captioning, transcripts, and written descriptions of visuals (or "alt text"). Confirm also that your platform and the slides you share through it will play well with other accessibility tools participants may use during your session such as screen readers that convert text to audio.

All of these situations come with barriers that can make it hard for your audience to stay focused on you. Being aware of that allows you to plan a presentation that's easier for them to enjoy and worth their time and effort. This includes choosing the best format for your virtual presentation, as we'll explore in the next chapter.

Choose Your Format

While analyzing your audience, you may have some thoughts about what you want to say and how you want to say it. But before you get going on writing or designing slides, you have one more strategic choice to make—the format of your virtual presentation. This involves anticipating how aligned (or not) your audience is with your idea and then deciding how you'll interact with them to get people on board.

Assess where your audience stands

Persuasive communication is a dynamic process. It begins when a person has a message to "send" and kicks things off, but it quickly becomes a give-and-take with the people who "receive" that message. If the sender and the receivers are pretty much on the same page, alignment will come quickly. Otherwise, the sender has some extra persuading work to do.

To move your audience closer to your way of thinking, you'll need to assess the gap you're trying to bridge. You can do that by anticipating the degree of resistance you expect to encounter. According to social judgement theory, people respond differently to ideas they find acceptable versus unacceptable.[31] Consider this spectrum when thinking about the content you will be sharing in your presentation: Is your audience likely to find it unacceptable, acceptable, or to view it in a neutral way *(Figure 6)*? The more unappealing the concept, the harder it will be to move people to share your beliefs. The effort required to move people will drive decisions about the format of your presentation.

FIGURE 6

Identify Where Your Audience Stands on Your Idea

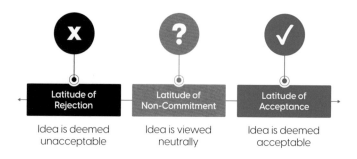

Decide how you will interact

If you think your audience is fairly close to agreeing with you, it might be fine to simply communicate information and not gather feedback. But if they are likely to be neutral at best or resistant at worst, you may need to warm them up to your idea by engaging them in dialogue about it. Or you may want to involve your audience in co-creation—have them actively generate ideas and suggest solutions to problems—to close a larger gap in mindsets or to persuade people to do something specific to help implement your idea. These choices about interactivity define how involved your audience will be, but they also put constraints on you, so pick carefully. You have three basic format options: linear, interactive, or collaborative *(Figure 7)*.

A **linear presentation** is what it sounds like—a presentation that follows a straight line from speaker to audience. This approach works best for times when you need to disseminate information to a large audience all at once without interruption, such as when you're making an announcement or giving people an update. It may be delivered as a live or pre-recorded webcast, featuring a slide presentation or video of the speaker talking (with simple props or without visuals of any kind). Usually, audience interaction is kept to a minimum, with the chat kept closed during the talk and just a brief Q&A at the end so there's little need for a moderator or technical producer. This type of presentation is faster for speakers to deliver, since they can get through their slides without interruption, but the downside is the audience can feel isolated from them. Because this format is not interactive, people's attention can easily wander, so you'll need to keep it short—under 30 minutes. Research shows that large audiences are especially likely to multi-task—they know their inattentiveness won't be noticed by the speaker.[32]

FIGURE 7

Virtual Presentation Formats: Linear, Interactive, and Collaborative

	Linear Presentation	Interactive Presentation	Collaborative Presentation
Flow of Ideas	One-way dissemination	Two-way dialogue	Multi-way co-creation
Presentation Format	**Webcast:** Pre-recorded or live presentation with low or no audience interaction	**Webinar:** Pre-recorded or live presentation with some audience interaction	**Workshop:** Live presentation with high audience interaction or co-creation
Typical Uses	Executive memos and "fireside chats", announcements/ updates, canned demos, explainer videos	Marketing seminars/webinars, sales presentations, panel discussions, live demos, all-hands meetings	Training classes, team meetings, brainstorms, working sessions
Audience Size	Hundreds to thousands of people	Dozens to hundreds of people	Two to a few dozen people

	Linear Presentation	Interactive Presentation	Collaborative Presentation
Interaction Tools	Speaker audio and video on	Speaker audio and video on	Speaker audio and/or video on
	Limited Q&A at end	Participant audio and/or video on only if called on by speaker	Participant audio and/or video on
	No participant audio or video	Periodic polls or pause for questions	Whiteboarding/annotation
	Closed chat	Moderated chat	Breakout rooms
			Fully open chat
Visual Aids	Slides	Slides	Slides or documents
	Videos	Videos	Digital whiteboards
	Props	Props	Physical whiteboards/flipcharts
Roles Needed	Presenter	Presenter and Moderator	Presenter and Technical Producer
Length of Time	Under 30 minutes	30 to 60 minutes	45 to 90 minutes

That means your presentation must quickly capture their focus and work hard to hold it, especially if your talk is pre-recorded and there's no way for people to interact with you.

An **interactive presentation** brings the audience into the fold by inviting two-way communication between them and the speaker. This approach is common in talks that are designed to immerse people in a topic and engage them at length—for instance, webinars, keynotes, participatory lectures, or panel discussions. The interactive presentation has several benefits: it gives your audience an outlet to ask questions or express concerns, it helps you gauge how well your message is landing, and it feels livelier than a one-way talk. However, audience interaction also adds time, so you'll need anywhere from 30 to 60 minutes. To hold your audience's attention for this long, you'll want to vary your visuals (slides, props, videos), interaction tools (polls, moderated chat discussions, Q&A), and even speakers (co-presenters or panelists). The more interactive the format, the more effort it will take to run the show. Vocal audiences can flood the chat or Q&A faster than you are able to respond. Enlist a moderator to monitor and manage audience feedback while you speak.

Finally, a **collaborative presentation** turns your audience into highly active participants. This approach can be used in meetings and work sessions with small groups of people to explore a problem, generate alternatives, build shared understanding, or make decisions together. The visual aids you use to facilitate the conversation can vary from pre-built slides to live-sketched visuals on digital or physical whiteboards, to working documents created in real time using web-based collaboration applications. The less polished, the better, because unfinished graphics will signal that your ideas are still in development and stretchy enough to accommodate your audience's ideas as well. You might even invite participants to co-create in groups by sending them into breakout rooms to work through a topic together and then report out when you all reconvene. To allow space for everyone to provide input, you'll have to expand your run-time to 45 minutes or as long as 90 minutes. If possible, bring a technical producer to help you launch interaction tools and keep the session on track.

Since virtual presentations exist on a continuum of interactivity—from low to high audience involvement— you can dial participation up or down as desired. We'll look at additional options for interactivity in the Story section of this book, beginning on page 59. Regardless of what approach you choose, every element of your presentation should work together to move your audience.

Communicate in Multiple Dimensions

Once you have considered your audience's needs and decided which format will serve them best, you're ready to start planning the virtual presentation itself. If the date of your talk is approaching fast, you may be tempted to cut prep time by repurposing a presentation you have delivered in person before. But resist that urge. Virtual presentations are different creatures altogether, because they are fundamentally two-dimensional. You can overcome that constraint by adding depth to your communication and enhancing your presence as a speaker to create a more memorable, engaging audience experience.

Break out of the flatlands

Think back to the last time you saw a really great presentation in person. What do you remember about the environment? Who was in the room? Did they react to the presentation in the same way you did? Even more important, what do you remember about the speaker? What did their voice sound like? How did they "work the room"? What did it feel like to be in their presence?

As you ponder those questions, you'll probably remember certain images, sounds, or feelings. You might even recall a high point in the talk, like when everyone laughed at an unexpected joke or went silent as the speaker told a sad story. Those memories stuck because your senses were stimulated and further heightened by the reactions of others in the room with you. When sharing a moment together, audiences feel a communal energy known as "collective effervescence,"[33] which can generate positive feelings and memories about that experience and the speaker who created it for them.

Now try to remember the last great virtual presentation you saw. What can you recall about it? Can you remember any specific sights, sounds, or feelings? Chances are the memory is duller, as if your mental image was converted from vivid color to bland gray. That's because digital communication lacks all of the sensory input and nonverbal interactions that allow speakers to express emotion and receive feedback through nuanced facial expressions and physical gestures. With the possible exception of virtual reality, digital tools like videoconferencing and meeting apps convert you into a two-dimensional image rather than the three-dimensional person you are, rendering you flatter than in real life and preventing others from feeling that they are in the same space with you.

This absence of palpable togetherness (or social presence, as it was originally called) became a problem in the late

1970s and early 1980s,[34] when videoconferencing and telepresence technologies were introduced in the workplace. Now it's regaining relevance with the increase in remote work, which can make it harder for people to create deep, authentic human interactions while communicating and collaborating from afar. Today, we could say the challenge is to establish virtual presence.

Numerous studies[35] show that people project and feel less virtual presence on purely text-based channels like chat or email, and more on channels that allow verbal and nonverbal communication through sound and/or video. You can easily add some depth by keeping both your camera and mic on during your presentation and further enhance your presence by using your face, body, and words to draw people in *(Figure 8)*. This takes self-awareness on your part, but it pays off.

The content of your verbal communication helps build intimacy. Using active, accessible, and personal language signals that you're speaking directly to (not at) your audience. Telling a personal story that reveals vulnerability can make you seem more approachable and relatable and establish a bond with your listeners. Your nonverbal communication can strengthen your connection with them as well. For instance, as you tell that story, invite them in by making eye contact through the camera and leaning forward in your chair. Or smile and hold your hands out wide in an open stance so your audience will feel welcomed and included.

FIGURE 8

Classic Communication Techniques That Build Virtual Presence

Verbal	Nonverbal
Adopting active rather than passive voice	Making direct eye contact
Addressing others personally ("you", "we", "us")	Leaning forward, smiling, nodding
Using accessible language (avoid jargon or insider terms)	Matching the tone, volume, pace of speech used by others
Telling a story that creates connection	Using inviting and open gestures

These techniques work in person, too, but they are especially valuable in virtual environments, where presence is more elusive. If the technology you use generates high-quality video and audio, it'll be almost like "being there."

Bring you and your visuals into harmony

In addition to boosting your virtual presence, an effective remote presentation brings everything your audience sees into an integrated, harmonious whole. When those elements cohere, the constraints of presenting digitally actually work to your advantage, allowing your message to come through clearly and making it easier for people to stay focused on you while you're delivering it.

At Duarte, our term for carefully curating the layers of information within the viewer's screen—the backdrop, the graphics, and the presenter—is the TriCast Method™ *(Figure 9)*. "Tri," of course, refers to the three layers, and "Cast" is short for "broadcast," since viewers take in the presentation all at once, much as they would a video feed on a television screen.

FIGURE 9

Three Layers of Information in a Virtual Presentation

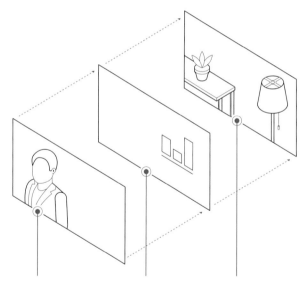

Presenter

- Who you are and how you look

- What you have to say

- How you say it verbally and nonverbally

Graphics

- What you show

- When you show it

- How it supports what you are saying

Backdrop

- Where you are speaking from

- What your environment says about you

- How it supports your message

The **backdrop** layer is what viewers see behind you. It shows the location you are speaking from, such as your workplace, your home office, or a professional studio, unless you decide to use a virtual background. It can also provide context about you and your topic. For instance, if you are delivering your presentation from corporate headquarters, you might position yourself in front of a wall that has your company logo or tagline on it. Or if you're an author, you might give your talk in front of a bookcase that holds some of your best-selling books. Select your backdrop with care. It will be behind you the whole time you're speaking, so it should be free of needless distractions.

The **graphics** layer (very broadly defined) includes any visuals that you show during your presentation, such as slides, whiteboards, or physical props. These help you establish a certain look for your talk, whether formal or casual. Also, your graphics must reinforce what you're saying without adding clutter. If there's too much dense text on your slides, your audience will stop looking at you and listening to your voice—they'll be too busy reading to focus on anything else. They'll be similarly distracted if your slides contain overly complicated diagrams or busy infographics that take extra mental effort to understand, so keep it simple.

The **presenter** layer is, of course, you, and what you have to say. Remember: The words you speak are only one aspect of your communication. How you conduct yourself while you're speaking—your facial expressions and gestures, and the volume, pace, and pitch of your voice—will also convey information to the audience. So will your wardrobe choices, which send little clues about who you are and what's important to you. Think about your personal brand and how you want to use it to express something intentional to your audience. Perhaps you save a signature outfit for high-stakes keynotes or wear a symbolic accessory that has meaning for you and the group of people you're addressing. These things should work together subtly to support your message.

Keeping the three layers integrated doesn't necessarily mean that you will always include content in all of them or that there's no hierarchy of elements. You will still need to make decisions about what to prioritize visually and when to do it (we'll discuss those decisions in the section on Visuals, beginning on page 93). Sometimes your backdrop might be a wall with nothing on it, or you might not share graphics at all. But even those are deliberate choices you can make to create a quiet space within your virtual presentation so the words you speak and the facial expressions you use connect with your audience.

03

Story

Craft Content That Holds Attention

In this busy world attention is hard to catch, and even harder to hold, especially in an online environment. Compelling content, rooted in storytelling principles, lures remote audiences away from their inboxes and keeps them engrossed in a virtual presentation.

A compelling virtual presentation starts with content that's sticky enough to keep your audience from wandering away as distractions pop up. Left to manage their own attention, how long will people stay with you before they begin to drift? At best, about the same amount of time it takes to hard-boil an egg.

To be more specific: Research on learning in educational settings found that students start to lose focus 10 minutes into a lecture. Savvy educators adapt by dividing 60-minute talks into 20-minute chunks and breaking *those* up with interactivity every 10 minutes.[36] The result: increased attention and retention of information.

Staying with the program is no easier for remote business audiences than it is for students in crowded lecture halls. One video streaming service reports only 25% of viewers will finish watching a pre-recorded video that's more than 20 minutes long.[37]

To hold your audience for the length of your virtual presentation, like an engaging professor can, craft captivating content that hooks and rehooks them throughout. That means serving up your ideas in consumable bites with a clear structure that's easy to follow, using a variety of content to cut through the noise in your audience's environment, and incorporating interactions that help people connect with you and your ideas.

Make Your Content Consumable

Attention spans are shortening, and that's affecting our content consumption patterns. A group of European social scientists studied data about consumers' use of content from a range of sources—including social media posts, Google Books, scientific publications, and movie ticket sales—and found that people become sated much faster than they used to.[38] For example, they found that the lifespan of trending Twitter hashtags decreased during the period from 2013 to 2016, and they observed similar patterns on other platforms.

"Content is increasing in volume, which exhausts our attention," one of the researchers explained, "and our urge for 'newness' causes us to collectively switch between topics more regularly."[39] These insights about our shrinking attention spans and hunger for novelty can help you craft a presentation people want to consume.

Keep it short

Effective virtual presenters don't overstay their welcome. In person you may have a *bit* more time and space to talk about a single topic. But a remote audience will lose interest especially fast if you go on at length, because more things are competing for their attention. In a virtual setting, shorter is sweeter.

Research conducted by Duarte in 2021 bears this out. In a survey of over 500 professionals in a variety of roles and industries, 64% of respondents said they prefer virtual presentations that are 30 minutes or less in length.[40] As interactivity increases, so does the ideal length of the presentation. Giving participants opportunities to ask questions or chat with the speaker will motivate them to stay focused longer.

Why do people want virtual presentations to be shorter overall? Our brains have limits. We can manage only so much information, or cognitive load, at one time. The more information we are given, the more it fills up our working memory, and when our working memory is filled too fast, we get overwhelmed and learning slows.[41] Receiving information in smaller units allows our brains to process and remember it. So rein in your length. It's a simple but effective way to improve the experience for your audience.

Serve up small bites, like a chef

Within your presentation, serve your content in bites that are easy to consume. This keeps audiences engaged for a couple of reasons. First, dicing up the information like this further reduces the risk of cognitive overload. Second, it gives you multiple opportunities to recapture your audience's attention, because each time you transition to a new bite, it'll register as novelty in people's brains. New things spark our interest and promote learning.[42]

Think of it this way: When you're creating a presentation, you're like a chef in a high-end restaurant that serves multi-course tasting menus. Your goal is to delight people by stimulating their senses throughout the meal. If you packed each plate with too much food, diners would lose their appetites, or get sick if they tried to eat everything. So instead, give people small, flavorful morsels that whet the appetite without overpowering it.

Pace yourself, like a scriptwriter

Film and TV producers have long understood that audiences have short attention spans and crave novelty. Scriptwriters pace themselves accordingly to keep viewers interested, with each scene lasting only a few minutes.[43] The script for a typical movie or TV show breaks the story down into three acts *(Figure 10)*. Within each of those building blocks, multiple scenes move the narrative forward—and each one must grab the audience, again and again, so they'll continue watching until the show is over.

FIGURE 10

How Television and Film Writers Build a Story

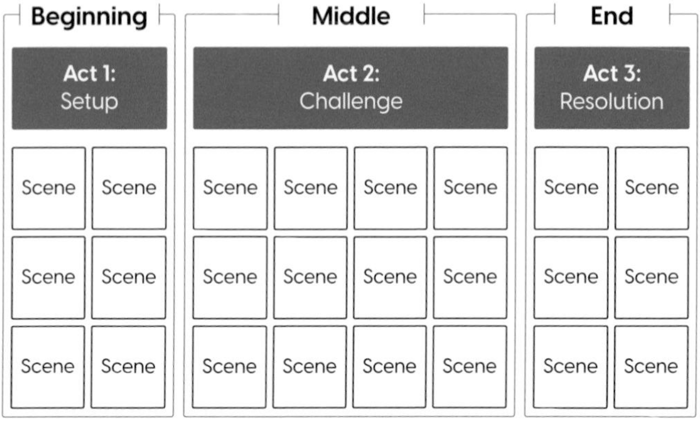

The three-act structure facilitates great storytelling. Act 1 is all about set-up: In the opening scenes, we meet the hero, learn about their goals, and discover the nature of the adventure that's about to unfold. The scenes in Act 2 are filled with challenges: The hero has to fight obstacles and overcome self-doubt as they pursue the thing they want most. Act 3 is the resolution: In the final scenes, challenges are worked through (sometimes happily, sometimes not), and the hero is changed in some way by the end.

Pace yourself like a scriptwriter when crafting content for your presentation (*Figure 11*). But in the "story" you're telling, the audience is the hero. When creating material for your first act, think of welcoming your attendees as "Scene 1" and setting the stage for their quest as "Scene 2," rather than lumping all opening remarks together into a blurry,

FIGURE 11

"Chunking" in a Virtual Presentation

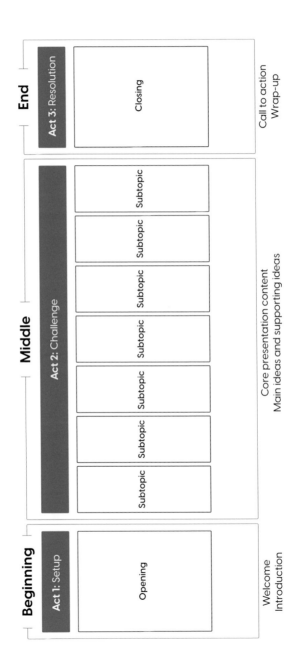

forgettable intro. In the middle, your second act, unpack your topic into a series of clearly defined subtopics that support your overall message. Throughout these scenes, you'll take your audience, step by step, on a journey toward your way of thinking. In your third act, wrap up with a call to action and key takeaways for your audience.

This approach to content creation, known as "chunking," works well for just about any type of presentation. But it's especially useful in virtual settings, because it breaks information into digestible bites that reduce overload and increase interest. The middle of the presentation may be the most challenging section to create, and not just because it's the longest. That's where you'll do the bulk of your persuasive work. If you don't unpack your topic in a way that continually reengages people, you'll lose them long before you get to the call to action.

What does unpacking look like in practice? Here's a quick example from a webinar I delivered on the importance of communicating well during times of change *(Figure 12)*. My goal was to educate my audience on what the journey of change looks like and how they should communicate at each stage of it. I began by establishing the case for change with a few brief slides describing the reasons organizations need to evolve and how it benefits their business. Then I segued into a section on why people resist change, which set the scene for my next sections: stages of the change journey and audience needs at each point along the way. Once I explained that journey, I introduced various communication tools that can

FIGURE 12

Structure of a Presentation on Change Communication

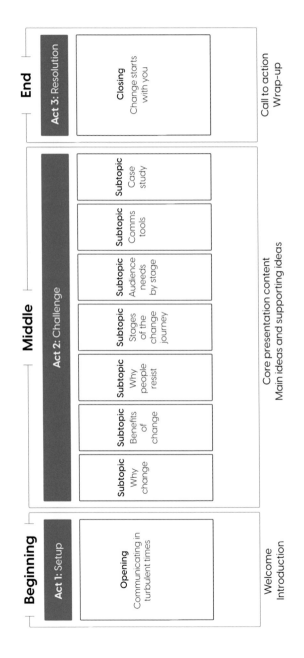

be used at each stage, followed by a case study of a company that navigated transformation successfully using the same techniques. Even within the case study, information was chunked to unveil the challenge, solution, and results. Finally, I closed with a rallying cry to inspire the audience to believe they, too, could lead change well using the techniques I'd shared.

This chunking technique, which is taught in Duarte's training courses, can be used across a set of presentations as well, like for a virtual event. An event program is essentially made of multiple chunks of content, often organized into tracks. Looking at content chunks this way can reveal larger themes to expand upon in other sessions at the event. For instance, if I were planning an event about leading change, I might create a track for leaders that dives into strategic case studies presented by executives who transformed their firms. Another track could be aimed at communication professionals who are tasked with crafting persuasive messages, with perhaps another track on the neuroscience of change for human resources teams. Across all sessions, stories about change would be a recurring thread that ties it all together.

Streamline your argument

Consumable content is also—perhaps above all—as focused as you want your audience to be. If your presentation strays, so will the people who are watching you. As you brainstorm the particulars of your talk, breaking information into small chunks helps you develop a cohesive argument. You can use paper index cards or sticky notes to write down potential topics and sketch out supporting points and data. That makes it easy to group the bits and pieces into related clusters and to begin placing them into the three basic sections—beginning, middle, or end—of your presentation. (Don't get too hung up on placement yet, though. You'll refine your structure later, using tips in the next chapter.) If you prefer to work digitally, you can use brainstorming apps or even presentation software, since slides are as modular and moveable as sticky notes.

However you capture your thoughts, if you're planning to share slides as you talk, limit yourself to one idea per slide so your audience will fully grasp each one.[44] Be concise when you're crafting your talking points, too, because short sentences are easy for listeners to digest. Even short words and phrases—"we're" instead of "we are"—save your audience time and effort (extra words add up!) and make your speech more conversational and engaging.

Fine-Tune Your Structure

It's time to finesse the overall structure and flow of your talk, and incorporate smooth transitions from topic to topic. By now, as discussed in the strategy section, you have chosen the virtual presentation format that best fits the moment—linear, interactive, or collaborative (as discussed in the Strategy section, beginning on page 35). Your format will drive your decisions about content structure.

Leverage story structure

If your presentation will be linear or only slightly interactive, with light audience involvement relegated to the very beginning or end, then you can organize it into a prescribed structure like a "Duarte Presentation Sparkline™" *(Figure 13)*.[45] This persuasive structure draws inspiration from cinematic and literary storytelling techniques for creating and resolving tension. The speaker repeatedly juxtaposes the current state ("what is") against the future state ("what could be"). This heightens drama by building and releasing tension again

FIGURE 13

Use Tension to Move Your Audience Toward a New Idea

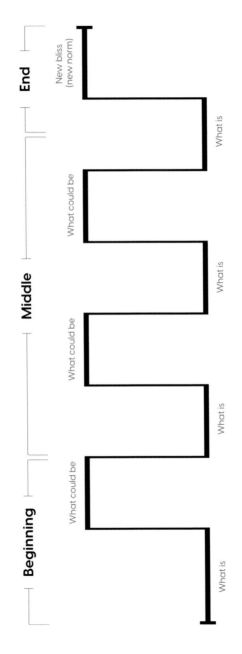

and again, keeping the audience on edge until the conflict between the status quo and the new way is resolved. Finally, the speaker closes by telling the audience how they'll benefit if they embrace the speaker's promise or vision, also known as the "new bliss." This powerful summary technique borrows storytelling principles to paint a picture of how the world will be better when your idea is adopted. But in an analytical or data-oriented narrative, the new bliss takes the form of a recommendation that will solve a problem or seize an opportunity.[46]

This persuasive structure can also be used to distinguish between problems and solutions, disadvantages and advantages, even questions and answers.[47] It's a great tool for overcoming resistance to an idea, as well, because you can dramatically address pros and cons rather than listing them as boring bullets on a slide.

Within a sparkline, stories can be used in several ways to keep your audience highly engaged *(Figure 14)*. One possibility is to use a single story at a discrete moment in your presentation. If you're announcing a new product, for example, you might incorporate a case study about a happy customer who was an early adopter. You could tell that story in the middle of your presentation, after you've described the problem the product was designed to solve. The story would help support your claims about the product's benefits and to add emotional appeal that will make its advantages more memorable.

FIGURE 14

Three Ways to Use Stories in a Linear Presentation

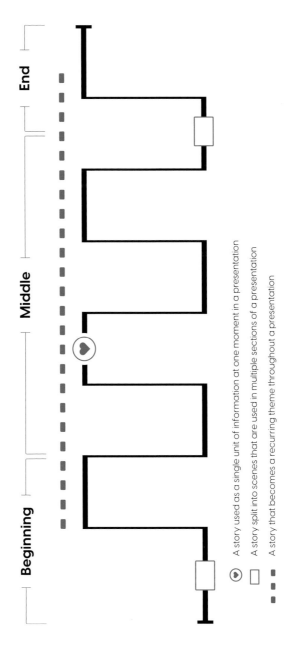

Beginning Middle End

A story used as a single unit of information at one moment in a presentation

A story split into scenes that are used in multiple sections of a presentation

A story that becomes a recurring theme throughout a presentation

Or you could divide that customer story into multiple scenes that appear at different points in your presentation. How might that work in the situation above? Start your talk by describing how a customer brought you a problem that inspired you to develop a new product. In the middle, unveil the new product and explain how you enlisted the customer to help test it out. Then, at the end, reveal how that product solved your customer's original problem and ultimately improved their business.

Another option is highlighting a central metaphor, detail, or image in a story and threading it throughout your presentation as a recurring theme that ties everything together. Perhaps that customer who came to you complained about trying to do "Space Age work" with "Stone Age tools" because the technology they were using before was so outdated. That analogy could become the overarching concept for a presentation where you'd explore how your product evolved to solve a new set of problems, just as human innovations evolved from the Stone Age to the Space Age.

Whatever approach you use, make sure your story is relevant to your content and relatable to your audience, or it might distract them from your main points.

Go with the flow

Highly interactive and collaborative presentations—like sales conversations, panel discussions, or workshops—need a more flexible structure that allows you to respond to input from the audience or other speakers. In these kinds of sessions, the content flows from multiple contributors who are all adding to the discussion. If the lead presenter and the rest of the group are largely in sync, the shape of the discussion may be fairly straightforward—moving from opening remarks into an exchange of ideas, and then advancing to a call for action. If participants are not aligned (as is often the case), the shape may be messier as people debate about the right course forward.

Even when perspectives diverge, you can apply a basic structure with a beginning, middle, and end. But the middle will have to be pliable to bend with the dialogue. At Duarte, we call this structure a "designed conversation" because it permits organic give-and-take while allowing the presenter to steer the dialogue with discussion prompts. Prompts could take the form of provocative statements, thought-provoking questions, or even stories *(Figure 15)*.

For example, to kick off a virtual workshop on leadership, you might tell a personal story about a key challenge you faced as a manager and then invite participants to share their own experiences in handling similar situations before you teach some coaching techniques to help them hone their management skills. Or if you're moderating a virtual panel discussion on diversity, equity, and inclusion, you might first frame up some common issues you want the group to examine and then tell a short story to illustrate what those can look like in an organization before passing the Zoom mic

FIGURE 15

Using Stories to Prompt Discussion in an Interactive or Collaborative Presentation

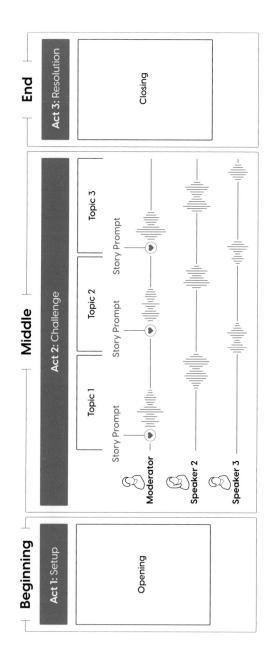

to your co-presenters. In a webinar on the same topic, after telling your story, you could ask people to type their reactions in the chat or invite several participants to turn on their mics to share stories before you propose a new way of thinking about inclusion in the workplace.

By nudging others to recall and share related tales from their own lives, story prompts can bring energy to collaborative presentations. Soon the stories will pop up like kernels of corn in a hot pan, and your virtual conversation will really be cooking.

Provide navigational cues

However you structure your content, make sure it's easy for your remote audience to follow, or they might become frustrated and tune out. Like markers on a map that say "you are here," visual cues can signal to an audience which section of the presentation you're in and what's coming next. An obvious approach is to include section breaks within your slide deck and use a different color or layout for those transition slides to show you're moving to a new topic. Or you can put icons or other wayfinding symbols on slides to indicate which subtopic or section you are covering next.

Verbal transitions also help signal that you're switching topics *(Figure 16)*. You can kick off your talk with a phrase like "To start…" or "Let's begin…," segue between topics with cues like "Next…" and "Moving on…," and lead into your closing points with "Finally…" or "To wrap up…" It also helps to embed mini recaps into your transition statements, such as "We've covered topic A and talked about topic B, so let's dive into topic C next…" as a way to remind your audience of what they've learned so far.

FIGURE 16

Verbal Transitions Between Sections

Beginning	Middle	Ending
"What I want to talk about is…"	"Next, I'd like to…"	"To wrap up, I want to …"
"My first topic today is…"	"Moving to the next topic…"	"Which leads me to my last topic…"
"To start, we'll explore…"	"Another thing to consider…"	"As a concluding thought…"
"Let's begin by…"	"Continuing on…"	"Finally…"

These standard-issue phrases—quickly uttered and easily understood—do a lot of navigational work without taking much space. But in some places, you'll want to push past the expected. Liven up some of your transitions by using a bit of suspense to build anticipation, as in "We've been working for a long time on this challenge and I'm excited to finally reveal how we've solved it…," or by posing rhetorical questions, as in "How will it all end? Let's find out now!" Questions are also a great way to draw your remote audience into a conversation with you, as we'll see in the chapter on orchestrating purposeful interactions.

Manage Their Distractibility

Holding your audience's attention from beginning to end takes work. Creating consumable bites of content and applying storytelling principles will help, but these aren't the only techniques at your disposal. You can also lure people in by actively managing their attentiveness. Sometimes that means cutting through the noise and the fog in your audience's environment so your message is what people hear and remember. And sometimes it involves using distraction itself as a tool, to prevent people from drifting off or to re-engage their interest once they've begun to wander.

Hook them early on

Remember those twitchy students whose minds start tuning out 10 minutes into a lecture? In reality, their attention is not only wandering but constantly waxing and waning. According to researchers at Princeton and UC Berkeley, the human mind is rarely focused as steadily and tightly as a spotlight. Instead, our attention pulses off and on, like a strobe light, as rapidly as four times per second.[48] That's because our brains are always scanning the environment for threats or opportunities, things we want to avoid or approach.[49]

If you build novelty into your virtual presentation from the start, your audience will be neurologically compelled to pay attention to the exciting new thing that caught their eyes or ears. Since novel experiences flood the brain with dopamine, the chemical associated with rewards and learning, you'll stimulate positive feelings and open up minds from the get-go—putting yourself in a better position to compete with environmental interference.[50]

Grabbing attention right away with a fresh turn of phrase, a surprising fact, or an unexpected observation—a device that writers call a "hook"—makes people want to dive in. When you begin your presentation, try to avoid the usual openers: "Hi, my name is _____ and I'm excited to talk to you about _____." Instead, share a startling statistic, an entertaining story, or a provocative quote to kick off your topic. Anything that's different from the intros your audience typically hears will pique their interest in listening to the rest. Plus, it'll make a strong first impression.

Hold attention with variety

Getting the audience hooked is only your first challenge, because their attention will still wander as your presentation unfolds. Engagement is often at its lowest point in the middle of a talk, after the initial novelty has worn off and the speaker settles into a predictable rhythm. You'll need to re-hook people throughout your talk by infusing variety into the midsection. Try mixing content types (stats, stories, quotes, analogies) and communication devices (charts, photos, videos, demos) when writing your presentation *(Figure 17)*.

FIGURE 17

Mix Up Your Content Types and Communication Formats

Type	Format
Numbers/statistics	Chart/graph
Analogies/metaphors	Illustration/photo/animation
Stories/testimonials	Video
Simulations/examples	Demonstration/performance
Statements/quotes	Text slide
Interview	Discussion
Technology explanation	Architecture diagram

For instance, when talking about a product, don't simply explain it in a series of bulleted slides. Consider using an example or analogy to describe how it works conceptually, then show an architecture diagram of how it works, followed by a live demo of the product in action, ending with a testimonial video of a customer gushing about why they love it so much. Contrast keeps people watching.

This is especially important when you're presenting data, which can be dense and mind-numbing. If you're presenting the results of a survey, highlight a revealing statistic on a simple number slide and then segue to a more detailed chart that backs up your claim. After that, you might tell a story about how you arrived at those insights, since facts paired with stories are often more memorable than facts alone.[51]

The key is to vary what you say and how you say it. When you unpack ideas in unexpected ways, you'll reward your audience for sticking with you and increase the chances that your messages will stick with them, too.

End on a strong note

When it's time to wrap up, finish on a strong note. A phenomenon known as the "primacy-recency effect" suggests that people can most easily remember the first thing(s) and the last thing(s) they heard.[52] So while it's important to hook your audience early in your talk, what you say in your close also has a greater chance of being recalled. Make the ending count.

Often speakers like to finish by summarizing their main messages, but the recency effect will still limit what an audience remembers most to the final points. So it's important to issue a clear call to action at the very end. That way, the thing you want the audience to do when your presentation is over will stay fresh in their minds. You can even use the virtual medium to coax people into taking that first step—for example, by asking them to write one thing they plan to do into the chat box. There are many more uses for the interaction tools in your virtual communication platform, which we'll explore next.

Orchestrate Purposeful Interactions

We live in a very vocal world. Thanks to social media, people have been trained to give a thumbs up or thumbs down to practically every piece of content that shows up in their feed. We get rewarded with a hit of dopamine when we post comments that garner likes or generate more chatter.[53] Because of this, online audiences have been conditioned to make their voices heard even when someone else has the floor. If you don't give them an appropriate outlet to communicate with you during your virtual presentation, they could disengage entirely. Conversely, if you do invite their feedback, they'll feel more connected to you and other participants. Plan to involve your audience early and often with purposeful interactions.

Match your tools to your situation

Research by the Goodman Center[54] found that "promoting interaction" was the third most-important quality in an online gathering, after providing engaging content and having a clear structure. Most virtual communication technologies are packed with features you can use to pull your audience into dialogue with you. These in-platform tools can be complemented or even replaced by out-of-platform tools from other applications like websites or mobile apps that your audiences can reach using QR codes on slides or links sent in advance.

When choosing your interaction tools, make sure they will be easy for you and your audience to use so moments of participation happen efficiently and don't disrupt your flow. Such tools can range from simple to moderate to complex, depending on the depth of interaction you want, the size of the audience you're addressing, and the level of effort required by everyone involved. To select the best method for engaging an audience, consider your goals for communicating with them and use that context to decide which tools fit the situation *(Figure 18)*. Many commonly available platforms have some or all of the capabilities listed here. However, virtual communication technologies are evolving all the time, so check for updates in your preferred platform before planning your next presentation.

Simple interactions take very little time to complete—a few seconds to click a reaction button or under a minute to answer a poll question—so they work well for quickly taking the pulse of a large number of people. But you won't glean deep insights from instant reactions. To go beyond surface-level impressions, you can ask participants to complete a longer survey after your presentation. Or encourage your

FIGURE 18

Interaction Tools and Their Uses in Virtual Presentations

	Simple Interaction *Check the pulse*	Moderate Interaction *Glean deeper insights*	Complex Interaction *Build connections*
Speaker Goals	Engaging a medium to large audience Taking a quick pulse of participants Keeping interactions short to save time	Engaging a small to medium audience Soliciting detailed feedback Provoking thought and discussion	Engaging a small audience Observing emotional reactions Building connections between participants
Audience Actions in Platform	Answering poll questions Using reaction buttons (thumbs up, hand raise, applause, emojis, etc.)	Reacting to speaker's slides using drawing features to annotate Putting comments into the chat or Q&A pane	Turning on microphone/camera to ask a question or make a comment verbally Participating in a breakout discussion
Audience Actions Outside of Platform	Filling out a form on a website Clicking to download slides/resources	Answering questions on a web-based polling tool Posting comments on social media site	Writing or doodling on digital whiteboards or physical paper Collaborating on a web-based document

audience to continue engaging with you by downloading slides and other resources when your talk is done.

Moderate interactions during a presentation involve detailed audience feedback via text-based chat or Q&A, visual annotation tools that allow participants to mark up the speaker's slides, or external web-based apps or social media sites. Such interactions give people opportunities to raise questions or make comments in their own words (or even drawings), allowing them to elaborate more than they could by responding to a basic poll. You'll learn more about your audience by giving them room to express themselves as you present, which means you can tailor your talk as you go. But you'll also consume more airtime, because you're asking people to think and then articulate those thoughts. For that reason, moderate interactions work best for somewhat longer presentations and small to medium audiences.

Complex interactions draw audience members into deep dialogue with you and with one another through immersive conversations or collaborative activities. For instance, you might ask participants to turn on their camera and/or mic to express their thoughts and feelings to the whole group or in a smaller breakout session. Maybe invite them to co-create with you by contributing ideas to a shared digital whiteboard or document, or by scribbling ideas on actual paper at their desks and then airing those thoughts with the group. Your agenda needs to allow space for each person to think and share, so these interactions are best for small groups and longer working sessions.

Inject energy by varying interactions

Once you decide what types of interactions you want and how they should unfold, build them into the flow of your presentation in a way that feels natural and aligned with your content. It's possible and beneficial to mix-and-match interaction types within a single presentation. Duarte's research[55] found that audiences enjoy all of these interactions equally well, with only modest differences. Alternating among simple, moderate, and complex interactions can make the audience experience more interesting. You'll add variety to your talk and boost the energy of your audience as they toggle from passive to active participants. It will also feel more inclusive because it allows people to contribute in the mode that fits their preferred communication style.

To understand how various interactions can be used, let's revisit the structure of the change communication webinar I mentioned earlier *(Figure 19)*.

Remembering that audiences can become distracted in 10 minutes or less, I usually plan an interaction in the first five minutes of my presentation. Because this webinar was about the challenges of inspiring people to embrace change, I wanted to get people thinking right away about a transformation effort they are involved in. I did this by posing an open-ended question on a slide and asking the audience to answer it in the chat box. As the answers flowed in, I commented on the patterns I saw and made mental notes about challenges I'd echo later in my talk.

FIGURE 19

Interactions in a Sample Virtual Presentation on Change Communication

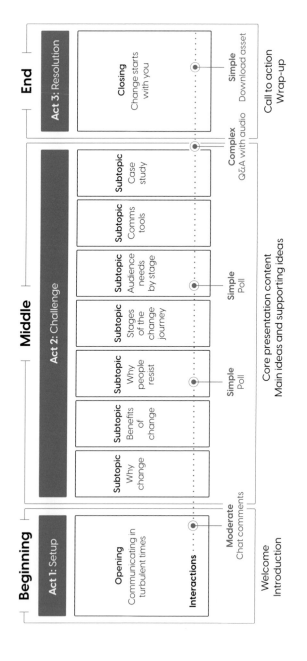

In the middle of my talk, I periodically paused to pose multiple-choice questions for the audience to answer using the in-app polling tool. Finally, I wrapped up with an open-ended Q&A discussion and then shared a link to a web page filled with resources to download later. This combination of activities gave my audience opportunities to share their thoughts with me and learn from their peers as they saw how others responded. In more collaborative situations, like workshops and working sessions, I lean heavily on complex interactions like whiteboarding and breakout discussions. But I'll still use a simple interaction in the beginning to break the ice and warm people up before I ask more of them.

Direct the action

Your audience won't know what you expect from them unless you tell them. To reduce uncertainty and help people prepare their minds, clearly spell out in the beginning how you want them to participate and which tools they'll use. If you will be incorporating out-of-platform tools like collaboration applications or SMS-based polls, participants might need to download software or sign up for access before the presentation begins. In those situations, include instructions and direct links within the event confirmation email or meeting invitation. But if you're using in-platform tools, you can simply explain how to use them when you begin the session. In Duarte's virtual training workshops, we do a combination of both: a short pre-workshop email with information about the platform we use and a reminder to download the latest software version, plus a quick orientation at the start of the meeting.

Communicate the audience norms you'd like to establish regarding use of attendee video and audio throughout the presentation. It's common for a host to announce at the start of a webcast or webinar that "all participants will be muted until the Q&A portion at the end." Or a facilitator of a small-group session can encourage attendees to "turn on your video cameras, because we'd like everyone to fully engage," but ask them to "please stay muted until it's time to ask questions or share ideas." Just know that some organizations have distinctly "camera on" or "camera off" cultures, so don't be offended if people don't turn on their video when you ask them to. And, while Duarte's research found that many people do in fact prefer the video camera to be on,[56] letting them choose if they want to be visible or invisible is empathetic.

During your presentation, remember to signal to the audience when it's time to contribute, which you can do easily with verbal cues like "Let's do a poll" or "Who has a question for me? Turn on your mic and share, please." It's also helpful to reinforce those instructions on the slides themselves—perhaps with an icon of a microphone when it's time for open discussion, or an icon of a pen on paper when it's time for annotation or whiteboarding. Posting instructions for complex interactions in the chat box provides extra clarity and saves time because participants can read directions on their own without having to ask you to repeat it all. Have instructions written out ahead of time so you or your producer can quickly paste them into the chat.

Speaking of chat, did I mention we live in a vocal world? If you're not actively moderating comments and responding to them, conversations happening in the chat can rapidly spin off in various directions. To stay focused on presenting your content, it helps to have a moderator or technical producer monitor comments and questions that come in, directly answer some of them, and keep track of others you should address during a Q&A at the end. Your moderator or producer can also launch polls and breakout rooms and post links to out-of-platform tools in the chat at prescribed moments. They'll have to be tech-savvy and agile problem-solvers who can handle an occasional glitch without getting flustered so the show can go on without interruption.

With your content and interactions planned out, you can begin thinking about the best way to support them with visual aids.

04

Visuals
Design for All
Dimensions

Virtual presentations have a lot in common with television shows and movies because everything that appears in the camera's field of view is a vehicle for conveying messages and emotions. When all visual elements work together harmoniously, the effect can be mesmerizing.

Well-designed visuals communicate ideas powerfully and accessibly. When they work in tandem with your words, audiences can better see what you're saying and make sense of it.

This effect can be explained by the theory of "dual coding,"[57] first described by psychologist Allan Paivio, who used brain science to investigate how people learn challenging concepts. His research revealed that words and graphics are each understood differently by the brain. Because these brain processes work simultaneously and support each other, messages are easier to process when accompanied by visuals.[58] As an added bonus, if those visuals are attractive or delightfully surprising, then the learning experience is more enjoyable,[59] an especially good thing in a virtual format, where it can be hard to keep audiences interested.

However, this dual-coding process works only when words and visuals clearly reinforce each other and don't compete for attention. Every dimension of what people see —including your backdrop, your visual aids, and you—must come together to form a cohesive visual experience for the audience. Think deeply about the best way to visualize your key messages and align every visual layer of your virtual presentation to support what you are saying.

Curate Your Backdrop

When you think of a virtual presentation, what sort of visuals come to mind? You may think of slides first because people often use them. They certainly are an important vehicle for conveying ideas, as we'll explore later in this section. But your viewers' eyes will also be drawn to other things, like your face while you're speaking and the background that's behind you.

While it may seem like only window dressing to you, your backdrop will speak loudly to your audience if it's particularly colorful, busy, or otherwise distracting. Make it work with you, not against you, by setting the right tone for your talk and subtly incorporating visual elements that fit your message and goals. You should curate your backdrop the way a director would set the scene for a film.

Learn the art of scene-setting

In filmmaking, designers are just as revered as writers for their craft, because they help bring the director's vision to life. They attend to every visual element, including costumes, makeup, props, and the sets the characters inhabit. Done well, set design builds a world so wondrous yet believable that it casts a spell on the audience, causing them to suspend disbelief and get swept away by the story. But if one visual element in a scene doesn't quite fit, it can break the spell and yank the audience back to reality.

That's why set designers obsess over every nuance in the background. Each detail adds to the audience's understanding of the story and the characters in it while conveying the right mood for that moment.[60] For instance, concert posters on the wall of a thirty-something movie character's living room say something about her interests. Later in the film, we might see the same young woman at work, backed by a wall of neatly framed certificates highlighting her professional accomplishments. In each scene, the physical environment communicates aspects of the character's personality so the audience will get to know her better and want to root for her.

You can have a similar impact on your audience by curating the backdrop for your virtual presentation as a set designer would decorate a room for a big movie scene. How? By making deliberate decisions about everything your audience sees. This includes the environment you're sitting in, whether that's your office at work or a workspace at home. Your audience will see what's on the walls, shelves, or tables behind you. Ask yourself if those details communicate something you want your audience to know about you—or if they convey an unintentional message.

Imagine you're that thirty-something movie heroine who's now interviewing for a new job. Of the two scenes we saw her in (living room and office), which would be most impressive to a prospective employer? Which details would make the employer feel more confident about her capabilities: the concert posters or the professional certificates? While this is a made-up example, similar scenes play out in our remote work environments all the time. A candidate who interviewed for a senior position at Duarte took the initial video call in his kitchen, where the recruiter saw towers of dirty dishes stacked on the counter behind him. The messy environment made a negative first impression, which could have been avoided if he'd taken the meeting in a different room or disguised it with a virtual backdrop. (Kitchens are fine for an appropriate purpose, by the way, like a cooking-themed virtual hangout with your team... but probably not for job interviews.) Being thoughtful about your background will help you set the stage for your virtual presentation and send the right message.

Match your environment to the moment

You can bring different levels of "polish" to your virtual presentations: casual, professional, or sophisticated *(Figure 20)*. The level you choose will drive your decisions about the visual environment around you.

A **casual** virtual presentation feels like a movie made at home by an uber-fan—full of heart but not full of bells and whistles. Its raw style gives off an authentic and approachable vibe that

FIGURE 20

Levels of Polish for Virtual Presentations

Casual If this were a film, it'd be a "fan" production	Professional If this were a film, it'd be an "indie" production	Sophisticated If this were a film, it'd be a "studio" production
Creative Approach	**Creative Approach**	**Creative Approach**
User-generated style of production	Business-ready style of production	Expert-level production
DIY visuals (handmade or minimalist graphics)	Polished visuals (professionally-designed slides)	Cinematic visuals (high-concept presentations)
Homey, "as is" real environment	Curated real environment or virtual background	Formal or virtual reality environment
Casual delivery	Polished delivery	Flawless delivery
Use Cases	**Use Cases**	**Use Cases**
Internal presentations and everyday updates	Customer or investor pitches	Launches and announcements
Working sessions	Marketing webinars	Customer or partner conferences
Video memos	All-hands meetings	Ceremonial events

fits informal communication like working sessions, project updates shared with colleagues, or quick video memos sent to employees. This style lends itself to a low-key setting, so letting people see your real home or office environment is totally appropriate. Appearing in your natural habitat will actually make you more relatable because objects in the room will tell people a story about who you are and what you have in common with them. You can even play to their interests by arranging these "artifacts"—for instance, giving an item with meaning to your audience (like a coffee mug with a local sports logo, or a symbol that's beloved in your company's culture) prominent placement in the scene.

Still, make sure your background is tidy, attractive, and free of visual distractions. To see it through your audience's eyes, snap a picture and send it to a friend with great taste who will provide honest feedback. Or log onto a virtual meeting and scrutinize what the video shows. Notice what draws your attention (crooked picture frames? a tangle of computer and printer cables on the table nearby?) and decide what to rearrange so it will be least distracting. For examples of what to do or not do with your backdrop, check out the Twitter feed for @RateMySkypeRoom,[61] a duo who got famous for giving honest reviews of the rooms used by people broadcasting from home.

A **professional** virtual presentation raises the quality bar. It's as if an indie director won a contract from a major studio and now has a bigger wallet—and bigger expectations. The extra investment is necessary for higher-stakes business situations like customer or investor pitches, all-hands meetings, or marketing webinars where brand image matters. In these situations, convey that you "mean business" with gravitas that reassures and impresses.

With that goal in mind, make sure your environment projects a professional image. This might require a change of venue. If it's convenient, go to your employer's office so everything looks top-notch. If you work from home, move your setup for the day to a suitably polished location in your house. Or upgrade your backdrop to a nicely designed virtual background like a slide with your company's logo or a photo of an iconic location from corporate headquarters. But avoid overly quirky or obviously fake scenes for this style of presentation—they can undermine credibility. In fact, respondents to a Duarte survey noted poor-quality fake backdrops as a top pet peeve in virtual presentations.[62] Some Duarte employees still opt to change their backgrounds to scenes from favorite movies or TV shows to create a festive atmosphere for team gatherings, but playful scenes are reserved for casual meetups, not customer pitches.

A **sophisticated** virtual presentation is the equivalent of a major studio film, where creativity can be boundless because the budget is large. You've got to "dress" your environment for the occasion to dazzle your audience and distinguish your brand from competitors. Such presentations include major product launches, annual conferences, and special ceremonial events (think awards galas, fundraising dinners, or centennial celebrations).

Audiences who tune into events like these expect to be wowed, so the "venue" needs to meet or exceed their expectations. Your sophisticated virtual presentation should feel as splashy as an in-person event in a grand hotel ballroom or a high-tech conference center. To match that quality, consider going to a broadcast studio equipped with TV-quality backdrops, cameras, lighting, and microphones. For extra-special effects, some virtual events are staged in a studio equipped with multiple green screens that surround the speaker to create a multidimensional canvas for displaying virtual reality and augmented reality graphics. Attaining this level of quality requires professional help from an expert design shop or a video production company, unless your employer is lucky enough to have that talent in-house.

Any of these options could be pre-recorded for on-demand viewing or delivered in real time to a live audience. But for very high-stakes situations, you may want to pre-record so you can edit out mistakes and edit in embellishments. Plan to allow at least 50% more rehearsal time for a virtual presentation than you normally would for a face-to-face presentation. That way you can fine-tune how you interact with your visuals.

Design Your Graphics

If you're going to use slides, as many presenters do, those visuals must reinforce what you're saying and engage the audience so they will understand and remember the messages you want them to take away. In a virtual medium, visuals have to work especially hard to accomplish all that.

Showing viewers where to focus is critical. Without guidance, people won't know where to look when taking in multiple streams of visual information at once. They may have trouble following along when two windows are vying for their attention—your slides in one window and you in another. Creating readable slides is also a high priority. People may struggle to make out all the details if they watch your virtual presentation on a small monitor or device. Avoiding predictability matters, as well. If your slides are repetitive, it gets boring quick. These challenges can be overcome if you apply principles of good design—like hierarchy, clarity, and contrast—when creating graphics for your virtual presentation.

Draw attention through hierarchy

During your virtual presentation, will people look at the images on your slides, or at your face? Or will they listen to your voice while looking at something else altogether, like their email? And when will their attention shift from one thing to another? You can direct their focus where you want it most at each moment by creating a deliberate hierarchy of visual elements, beginning with what "view" you provide for the audience. Many virtual communication platforms offer multiple options, and each has its pros and cons *(Figure 21)*.

One option is to share a **single** view with your audience, by showing only your slides while keeping your video camera off or by showing only your video with no slides. The main benefit of this singular view is that it lets your audience focus their eyes on just one thing so they can deeply immerse themselves in your ideas without having to split their attention.

Going the video-only route will feel more intimate than slides-only, and it's easier to produce—you can devote your energy to refining your script without having to worry about creating graphics. Beware, however, of letting low effort lull you into complacency. A video-only approach can be lackluster if your content isn't compelling, or your speaking style is subdued. Having some type of visual aid is especially important for presentations involving highly conceptual or complex content that needs to be seen to be understood, such as product overviews or financial updates. In those cases, you can share detailed slides but keep your video off so the graphics will be as large as possible.

FIGURE 21

"View" Options on Virtual Platforms

Single: One channel is viewed primarily

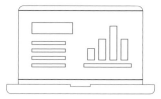

Presenter with no slides

Slides with no presenter video

Pros

Fast and easy for presenter to create (no visuals required)

Sets intimate, casual tone

Puts focus squarely on the speaker and their delivery

Pros

Familiar to presenters who frequently use screensharing apps

Conveys messages clearly through visual aids

Draws audience's eyes to slides

Hides presenter backdrop

Cons

Can be distracting if presenter's environment is cluttered or their appearance is not polished

Feels lackluster if presenter is not naturally dynamic or if their delivery is flat

Cons

Common format lacks novelty

Lessens connection by eliminating speaker expressions/gestures

Requires more prep time by speaker to create slides

Concurrent: Two channels are viewed simultaneously

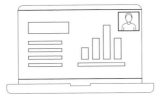 

Slides large, presenter small   **Presenter and slides equal**

Pros

Familiar to presenters
who frequently use
screensharing apps

Adds slightly more personal
touch with presenter video

Draws audience's
eyes to slides

Backdrop is less important

Pros

Familiar to users of
livestream apps that allow
multiple video feeds to be
shared at once

Draws audience's eyes to
both slides and speaker

Cons

Reduces visual weight of
speaker and impact of
expressions/gestures

Cons

Splits audience
attention between
slides and speaker

May lead to information
overload if slides are too
densely packed

Fused: All channels are viewed in a fully-integrated way

Presenter with slides as backdrop

Presenter and graphics on same plane

Pros

Mimics face-to-face presentation by placing slides behind speaker

Allows speaker to interact with visuals

Slides can be scaled up or down in size relative to presenter

Easier for audience to follow slides and speaker at once

Pros

Gives audience fewer things to focus on—speaker plus simplified graphics

Elevates the overall experience with TV-like production quality

Easier for audience to follow slides and speaker at once

Cons

Doesn't work with all slide layouts; requires re-design to allow space for speaker video on top of slide

Requires speaker to rehearse delivery so they can refer to slides without breaking eye contact with the audience for too long

Cons

Requires sophisticated graphic design and video editing skills

Demands more prep time by speaker to master interaction with visuals

Remember, though, that people can't read text and listen to you at the same time. You'll need to give your audience time to absorb what's on your slide before beginning your verbal explanation. And even if you do that, a slides-only presentation has a downside: you lose the ability to form a connection with your audience through eye contact and facial expressions. The overall effect can feel colder than video-on communication, which may be why only 4% of respondents to a Duarte survey prefer presentations where the speaker's video is off.[63]

Your communication can be richer if you share two information channels at once, in a **concurrent** view. This is the default format in screensharing applications, which launch slides in one window and speaker video in another, so it's familiar to most presenters. It's also familiar to business-to-business audiences because it's often used in presentations like sales pitches, live demos, and marketing webinars.

A concurrent view feels slightly more personal than slides-only, since the audience can still see the presenter's face. But on screensharing apps, the slide window is often visually dominant, taking up a larger portion of the viewer's screen. Some virtual communication platforms allow viewers to resize those windows, but not all do. As a result, the visual weight of the speaker's expressions and gestures is diminished. This proportion issue is partially resolved if you use a platform that's designed for livestreaming video content, which allows video windows to be larger. Still, the audience will have to watch two streams of information simultaneously—your video and your slides—so make sure your slides are readable and clutter-free.

The most cohesive visual experience can be created with a **fused** view that fully integrates the presenter and the visuals on a single plane. Some virtual communication platforms make this possible by allowing presenters to turn a slide presentation into a virtual background. The effect mimics face-to-face presentations where the speaker stands in front of a giant screen, allowing audience members' eyes to simultaneously watch the presenter and the slides without glancing back and forth. Even better, presenters can interact directly with virtual slides like a newscaster who reports on the weather, using their hands to point to specific areas they want the audience to notice.

If you don't have a remote communication tool that enables the fusing of speaker video and images, you can hire a video production company to integrate them using high-end editing tools. You'll get a final product that looks more like a TV show than a presentation. Whether the fusing is automated or professionally done, be sure to rehearse how you interact with your visuals while maintaining eye contact to build rapport with your audience.

Enhance impact with clarity and contrast

The next step in creating visual hierarchy is to bring clarity to your slides themselves so your audience's attention is drawn to the most important information being shared on screen. Viewers shouldn't have to sort through multiple ideas on one slide to figure out your main point. Stripping your slides down to the most essential information will guide their focus and make it easier for you to speak to them without losing eye contact. To keep things simple, remember this rule: include only one idea on each slide.

Begin by analyzing your slides to determine what's necessary and what isn't. A good way to gauge what will stand out most to your audience is to do a "glance test."[64] First, open your presentation and put it into slideshow mode. Then glance at each slide for three seconds, one at a time. If you can grasp what a slide is about that quickly, without scrambling to remember what you meant to convey, it passed the test. If not, trim the content. Ask yourself, "What's the *one thing* I want my audience to take away from this slide?" If you stuck to the "one-idea-per-slide" rule when writing content, you've got a good foundation to work with as you move into design.

But if extra information crept in as you built your deck— and you ended up with bulleted lists or multiple charts and graphics on a single slide—you've got some culling to do. Eliminate extra text or busy visual elements and make purposeful design decisions that allow your ideas to shine brightly. At Duarte, we call this giving your slides a "S.P.A. Treatment™": *simplifying, planning,* and *accentuating* all the elements to create a pleasing visual experience *(Figure 22)*.

FIGURE 22

Clarify Slides With a S.P.A. Treatment™

Simplify: Cut the clutter

Market Overview: Revenue By Industry and Quarter

· Manufacturing and retail are the strongest industries, generating 75% of revenue
· Revenue started low in Q1 but trended upward in Q2, Q3, and Q4 set a new record
Revenue is strong across industries with more growth potential to be tapped

Before

Quarterly Revenue

Revenue grew from Q1 through Q4

Q4 was our biggest yet

After

Plan: Reimagine the slide

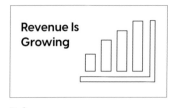

Quarterly Revenue

Revenue is growing

Before

Revenue Is Growing

After

Accentuate: Use design with purpose

Revenue Is Growing

Before

Record Growth

$5M

Q4

After

First, **simplify** your visuals by removing everything except the most essential information required to communicate the main idea on each slide. For instance, you might put multiple charts onto separate slides and move wordy descriptions into notes that you will say rather than show. This step is critical if you want to use your slides as a virtual background, because you'll need to clear space beside each graphic to make room for your video to appear there. When you need to show a complex diagram, make the graphic as large as possible so the audience can carefully read and process the details. You can let that diagram fill the screen, stepping out of camera view (or skooching your chair to the side) long enough to let viewers read the full slide without obstruction. Similarly, edit the text that remains on your slides to make it as short as possible and yet still convey meaning. For visuals that can be read at a glance, aim for five to seven words per slide. If you can't bear to let go of all your words, consider creating a companion document—or Slidedoc™—that includes a detailed narrative for each slide that attendees can read later to get the deep-dive.[65]

Second, **plan** how best to convey the information that's left by exploring different ways to visualize your ideas. Consider choosing a different chart type to display your data or turning words into visual concepts and metaphors to drive a point home. At this point, you should also enlarge the remaining text to be sure it's readable on the smallest, simplest device that your audience might be using to view your presentation. A general rule of thumb is: as screen size goes down, font size goes up.[66] For slides seen primarily on laptops or larger monitors, you can get away with a font size of 24 points. But if slides will be seen on a mobile device, the font will need to be somewhat larger. In a small test done by Chariti Canny, an art director at Duarte, a font size of 32 points was more comfortable for people who were reading text slides on a mobile phone. To check legibility of your slides on a mobile device, open your presentation on your smartphone to see whether you can read the text easily without having to zoom in. If not, try enlarging the font and view it again.

Third, **accentuate** the right elements on your slide for maximum impact, using contrast to direct the audience's attention where you want it to go. If you're displaying a bar chart, for example, highlight key data points with color or bold typography and perhaps add a text callout (or "annotation"), to underscore the message. By making information stand out from the background, you will also improve the readability of your slides. This is especially critical for audience members who are color-blind or vision-impaired, as highly-contrasting colors will make text more legible. To check the level of contrast, view your slides in "grayscale" mode—either by selecting that option within the slide-making app you're using or by printing a copy of your document with the output option of grayscale selected.

You can use contrast to hold attention, as well, by adding visual variety to your slides *(Figure 23)*. Changes in scenery will keep your audience interested. Instead of placing the same type of graphic on every slide, you might incorporate some photos or illustrations. Perhaps the background color in one section is blue while another section uses a green background. Even text-based slides can bring visual novelty to a presentation if you occasionally vary the text layout—for instance, by sprinkling in some slides with just a large phrase or a short statement instead of bullets. But you should still use a coherent set of elements throughout your deck—like the same typeface family, a common color palette, and a consistent grid—to visually ground your content in a signature look.

FIGURE 23

Vary Your Slide Types

Another way to add contrast to your virtual presentation is to use a surprising visual aid. Author Michael Bungay Stanier, known for his creative approach to presenting, often uses hand-drawn visuals like flipcharts. When speaking virtually, Bungay Stanier doesn't let go of analog techniques he's found effective in person, and the effect is charming. In one virtual keynote I watched, he wrote his main points onto sticky notes with a black Sharpie pen *(Figure 24)*, which stood out simply because it was so different from the polished slides other speakers use.[67] If you plan to handle props when you speak, just practice a bit until you're comfortable.

FIGURE 24

Hand-Drawn Visuals Can Surprise Virtual Audiences

Plan Your Presence

All three layers of a virtual presentation—your backdrop, your graphics, and you—must work together. So before you work on the mechanics of delivery (which we'll cover in the next section), think of yourself as one more visual element to design. This means working out how you will interact with your background and your slides to create a seamless visual experience for your audience.

Pick your posture

When presenting in person, you're free to roam about the room or stage as long as you stay within your audience's line of sight. The same is true in a virtual setting, but you can't roam nearly as far, since the audience's view is limited to what your camera shows. You'll want to stay inside that frame at all times.

As you do so, your main goal is to stay focused on the camera. That means your camera height will depend on whether you are going to sit or stand. Sitting is appropriate for a casual presentation or a collaborative session. However, a super-cushy chair might tempt you to slump forward a bit, which could muffle your voice. If you're going to sit, choose a chair that will encourage you to straighten your back so your voice will carry when it's time to deliver your talk. To be heard in your virtual presentation, you'll have to project your voice at a slightly higher volume than you would in a casual conversation. Your posture makes a difference.

You may equate sitting with comfort and security, but standing has its benefits, too. Standing will make you feel as if you're on stage, nudging your performance up a level in formality and polish. Being upright will also increase blood flow and thus energy, giving you a more commanding presence. Plus, you'll be able to speak from your diaphragm more easily than you would if you were seated, making your voice come out stronger.

Compose the shot

Next, determine where your face and body will appear within the scene you are composing for your audience. In the movie world, this is called "framing."[68] By planning where actors will stand within the visual frame, the director controls where the audience's eyes will go.

You can do the same by applying the "rule of thirds," a principle used in filmmaking and photography to compose images that are visually pleasing *(Figure 25)*.[69]

FIGURE 25

Apply the Rule of Thirds for a Well-Composed Image

Visualize
Imagine a
grid containing
9 squares

Align
Position yourself
within the grid—
centered without
graphics or
off-center with
graphics—while
keeping your eyes
in the top third of
the grid

When planning a shot, a cinematographer or photographer will structure it against an imaginary grid that divides the scene or image into nine boxes. Because nine is an uneven, or asymmetrical, number, it adds dynamism to the grid and to any image that's aligned to it. The places where the lines intersect are called "power points" that pull the eye in.

The rule of thirds helps determine where to position yourself in a virtual presentation, too. The most important visual element in a scene should be placed along those power points, because that's where the viewer's attention will go. If you are presenting using a "single" or "concurrent" view, where you and your slides will be in separate windows, then your body should be centered in the frame, with your eyes in the top third. That way, your face will remain the main focal point throughout your presentation. If you will use your slides as a virtual backdrop or have graphics placed around you by a video editor, you and your graphics will be "fused" within the frame. In that case, keep your eyes within the top third, but move your body to the side to allow space for your graphics to appear.

As you're looking at yourself in the frame, make sure any hand gestures you want your audience to see will be visible within the frame as well. Test this by logging onto a virtual meeting by yourself and turning on your camera, as you did to check your background for crooked picture frames and other distractions. Practice making some hand gestures as you speak. If the hand gestures you are making aren't visible on screen, try raising your hands up a bit higher, closer to your face but not covering it. Of course, this applies only when you're meant to be in view—not when you step aside so your visuals can take center stage. To make sure you stay in the right position while you speak, put colored tape on the floor where your feet should be in the "home" position in front of the camera. If you intend to sometimes walk "off stage" to let a slide fill the screen, then put another piece of tape on the floor to mark a place to the side where you'll stand out of the camera's view.

Dress for the occasion

Just as you would for an in-person event, choose your outfit carefully for a virtual presentation. Your clothing is one of the first things your audience will see, making an immediate impression. It tells people something about your personality and may even shed light on your profession. It can also convey how you feel about your audience—whether you respect them, for instance, or want to establish common ground. Match your attire to the way you want your audience to perceive you, while still being true to yourself.

For instance, your attire should match the level of polish your audience will expect—casual, professional, or sophisticated. For a team meeting, you might select a "business casual" outfit, such as a shirt with buttons. Dress it up a bit for a webinar, perhaps donning a blazer to bring added polish to your look. The extra panache could give you a psychological boost, too. When I'll be giving the main keynote at a formal virtual event, I wear high heels to remind myself to bring the same "A game" I'd bring to a big stage. Even though the audience can't see my snazzy kicks, they make me feel taller and slimmer, so why not? The same argument can be made for wearing slacks instead of sweatpants even though the online audience can't see your lower half. Personally, I save loungewear for the end of my workday as a treat to enjoy— along with a tasty beverage—after my presentations are done. But your mantra may be "business on the top, party on the bottom," and I won't judge you for that. To each their own!

What's considered appropriate will vary by audience, so do a bit of research on what they wear for remote work to avoid overdressing or underdressing according to their norms. When I started my career at a boutique consulting firm in the 1990s, my colleagues and I would wear suits to meet with clients. But when I showed up in my fancy suit and three-inch heels for a presentation at a tech startup, I knew I was out of place as soon as I saw the execs were clad in T-shirts and jeans. If I had done some research on startup culture, I would have discovered that "business casual" meant looking like a college student, not a young professional. Still, I didn't want to undermine my authority as a consultant, so it would have been in my best interest to dress *slightly* more buttoned-up than the group I was addressing. I made a mental note that next time, slacks, flats, and a tasteful blouse would be more fitting.

Speaking of fitting, make sure your clothes are the right size, too. You may think this goes without saying. But an executive I know recently conducted a virtual interview with a candidate who was dressed in a loud plaid shirt that was a few sizes too small. The candidate had been told to "come prepared as if you're selling to a CEO," but to no avail. When he gestured, his shirt strained at the buttons, and his chest hairs peeked through the gaps. A quick check in the mirror or on video with an objective eye could have helped him land the gig.

FIGURE 26

Your Wardrobe Should Complement Your Graphics

Do

Wear a darker wardrobe against a light background to show contrast

Wear a lighter wardrobe against a dark background to show contrast

Don't

Do not wear clothing that blends into your background

Do not wear patterns that can be visually distracting

Finally, select clothing that will complement your graphics *(Figure 26)*. For instance, you could choose a color that ties to your brand, such as a shirt in your company's branded shade of blue or a blazer that picks up your product's red hue. But avoid wearing colors that blend into your background—like a gray shirt against a gray slide or a green shirt against a green screen (unless you want to disappear!).

To minimize the number of colors or patterns that your audience has to process, stay away from clothes with busy designs or shiny fabrics because they will generate visual noise that distracts people. Solid colors with no patterns work best for presentations where the graphics will change often. Once you've planned out your background, graphics, and look, it's time to get ready to deliver with style.

05

Delivery
Command the Virtual Room

Engaging online audiences is an art that can be mastered with practice. By adapting your delivery style to the medium and fine-tuning all aspects of your virtual presence, you can create moments of connection that viewers won't soon forget.

You've nailed your content and your visuals, so you're ready to work on delivery. You may be tempted to cut yourself some slack when presenting online because it can feel like a lower-stakes setting than standing on a stage, facing a room of real, live people. But to keep your viewers interested, you'll have to put your best self forward. Your audience is the reason you've worked so hard up to this point to create a great presentation, and now it's time to bring it to life for them.

Every aspect of delivery is important in a virtual presentation, including your setup: the room you speak from, the atmosphere you create there, and the technology you use to engage people when you're speaking. The space where you deliver your talk must be outfitted with all the tools you'll need to be successful. We'll talk about how to set yourself up to present flawlessly, whether it's a casual situation or something more formal.

We'll also discuss the mechanics of delivery—voice and body—and how they create impact. Having coached thousands of speakers, Duarte identified three core traits of a powerful presenter: A *comfortable* speaker is well-prepared, physically at ease, and projects confidence. A *dynamic* speaker holds attention with vocal variety, gestures, and movement. An *empathetic* speaker identifies with the audience's needs and conveys that understanding through eye contact, effective pace, and responsiveness. These traits, many of which you'll learn here, are critical in a virtual setting, where an already-distracted audience requires incentives to stay focused.

Step Up Your Setup

When you deliver an in-person presentation, the atmosphere of the room matters. How the seating is configured, what the stage looks like, where the slides are shown—all these factors affect the audience's experience. Going virtual turns your home or work office into an event venue. The room you present from serves two purposes. First, as discussed in the section on visuals, it functions as the backdrop while you're speaking, quietly complementing your message. Second, it becomes your behind-the-scenes virtual broadcasting studio, allowing you to transmit your presentation clearly and persuasively. In this chapter, we'll focus on making sure your space serves that second purpose well. This involves situating yourself in a sound-friendly room and softening or silencing ambient noises *(Figure 27)*.

Situate yourself in a quiet space

Ideally, the room where you present will be free of background noise. People who work from home tend to be forgiving because we've all had to mute ourselves when a siren whined by or a dog barked unexpectedly. Hearing pets and kids can actually help team members bond and can humanize the people who manage them, so don't stress too much about those sounds in an everyday meeting. But for more formal situations, like conference presentations and pitches to the executive team, you'll want to avoid auditory distractions that might make it hard for your audience to stay focused on your message or hear your words at all.

FIGURE 27

Three Steps to Create a Sound-Friendly Room

Situate	Soften	Silence
Find a quiet, interruption-free room to present in	Add sound-dampening and noise-cancelling features	Remove or turn-off predictable sources of noise
Choose a space that's far from interior or exterior noises	Cover hard floors with rugs or hang sound-absorbers on walls	Turn off or mute any un-needed electronic devices
Close windows and doors	Leverage noise-cancelling features of your technology	Close out apps that emit alerts
Hang a "do not disturb" or "recording in progress" sign	Use a small fan, space heater, or white noise machine	Remove jewelry or accessories on clothing that might create extra noise

That means you'll want to deliver your talk from a room that's far from the din inside or outside your home or office building. This may seem like common sense, yet if you're like me, you've attended more than one virtual gathering that was interrupted by unexpected background noise. To prevent disturbances, choose a secluded location, away from areas that tend to get raucous—places where people chat, do chores, watch TV, or play. If you don't have many rooms to choose from and can't avoid being near loud spots, close windows and doors while you're speaking to keep the racket out. Or try presenting from a tidy closet (or "cloffice"), if you have one with enough space and light, because the clothing around you will help dampen noise.[70] Wherever you situate yourself, take a cue from TV and film producers and hang a sign on your door that reads "do not disturb—recording in progress" to discourage anyone from interrupting your performance.

Soften ambient sounds you can't prevent

Virtual communication technology is getting better every day, and some applications have built-in noise-cancelling features, as do good-quality microphones. But unwanted noise can still creep in from your environment itself if the space has a tendency to echo or if your housemates have very loud voices. To compensate, add extra sound-absorbing features to the room. This is particularly important if the room you need to use has floors made of wood or concrete, blank walls, or high ceilings. Those surfaces cause sound to reverberate, making it seem as if you are speaking in a can. Prevent this problem by decorating your space with soft furnishings and materials: a cushy couch or chair, curtains over the windows, rugs or blankets on the floor, or fabric artwork on the walls (good thing macramé is back in style). If re-decorating isn't in your budget, grab some couch cushions or bed pillows to scatter on the floor, out of the camera's view.

These fixes should be sufficient to satisfy everyday needs, unless you're a professional speaker. In that case, you might invest in acoustic panels to hang on your walls that give the room a radio-quality hush. Consider also upgrading the door to your room from a hollow model to one made of solid wood that will further dampen noise (especially if you have some very spirited children or pets). You might also consider placing a small fan or "white noise" machine on the floor to cancel out any other environmental sounds.

Silence the sounds you can predict

The last thing you want is for anyone—you or your audience —to get sidetracked by a flurry of alerts coming into your inbox as you present. To avoid this, turn off or mute devices you're not actively using during a presentation, such as your tablet or your mobile or home phone. Also, shut down or mute all apps besides your main virtual communication platform, like email and instant messaging, so none of them chime in when you're making a key point.

The same goes for jewelry or accessories (cufflinks, buckles, zippers, necklaces, etc.) that could jangle or bang against your microphone or desk while you move. Remove them. Once during a virtual presentation, I wore a favorite pair of dangly earrings that looked smashing with my blouse but clinked against the audio earbuds I was also wearing. This went on for several minutes without me noticing until I glanced down at the chat pane on my screen long enough to see a snarky comment from an audience member who'd had enough of the clamor. Mortified, I apologized briefly while pulling off my earrings, then resumed the talk a little pinker-faced than before. The unhappy situation might have been avoided if I'd done a brief tech check with my co-workers that morning, with earrings on, to make sure nothing was auditorily off.

Optimize Your Tech

Virtual presentations by definition depend on technology to transmit your video and slides to a remote audience. You can present online using the same tools you use every day for work—a laptop and a reliable internet connection—and it'll be sufficient for casual situations. But adding a few high-quality peripherals will take your presenting game to another tier. Using them properly will help you look sharp, sound strong, and feel confident. The upgrades don't have to cost a fortune, either, if you just choose the tools that will have the greatest impact on your output.

Gear up or down to suit your needs

Being a speaker in a virtual environment is a bit like being your own event producer. You not only have to present; you also have to choose and wrangle your presentation technology. Not every presentation requires the same type of tech. Duarte's event teams travel the globe working on splashy keynotes for global brands, where huge ballrooms are outfitted with massive LED displays, multi-color lighting rigs, and professional crews of sound, video, and lighting experts. But most presentations will be well served by a more modest setup. For example, a workshop in a small meeting room needs nothing more than a projector, a screen, and maybe a lapel mic for the speaker. In the same way, virtual presentation technology can be scaled up or down to fit your situation. Remember the three levels of polish we discussed earlier? Each scenario—casual, professional, or sophisticated—calls for different gear *(Figure 28)*.

A casual setup can be achieved with basic, consumer-quality equipment. The bedrock is a fast and reliable internet connection. For run-of-the-mill remote work, you can get by with strong Wi-Fi, but if you plan to share slides while also having your video on, hardwire into your internet access point with an Ethernet cable. Use an equally speedy and dependable computer with enough processing power to handle high-resolution graphics and large files. For improved audio, plug an external input source like a headset or mic'd earbuds into your computer to capture your voice with consistent quality. (Avoid wireless earbuds which are prone to cutting out if there's interference from another wireless device nearby or if the batteries die.) Finally, because the light emitted by your computer screen is an unnatural blue, you'll need good overhead lighting plus soft supplemental lighting for your face, either from a small lamp on your desk or a portable ring light. Don't rely only on sunlight coming through a window, because it won't be balanced and may cast garish shadows on your face.

FIGURE 28

Technology Needs for Virtual Presentations

Casual
Consumer-quality

Computer
Fast machine with lots of power and storage; if laptop with built-in camera, raise at least 6″ to keep lens at eye level, plus a clicker if you stand while presenting

Internet
A strong, reliable connection; ideally hardwired but wireless will do in a pinch

Microphone
Headset or earbuds plugged into your computer

Lighting
Soft overhead lighting, plus optional small desk lamp for fill lighting

Professional
Prosumer-quality

Computer
Same quality as a casual setup

Internet
Hardwired connection

Microphone
Headset, earbuds or standalone microphone plugged into your computer

Lighting
Desk lamp plus ring-shaped LED light mounted on monitor

Second monitor
Medium-sized external monitor to display secondary information

Webcam
Small external camera mounted atop external monitor

Green screen
Small portable green screen

Sophisticated
Expert-quality

Computer
Same quality as casual setup or faster processor for larger presentation files

Internet
Hardwired connection

Microphone
External standing microphone or lapel mic plugged into laptop

Lighting
Multiple lights, mounted on separate stands in a "three-point" configuration

Second monitor
Large wall-mounted monitor to display secondary information

Digital camera
Camera with video capture capability (like a DSLR) mounted on tripod

Green screen
Larger green screen

Optional: teleprompter screen for scrolling script separate from slides

A professional setup takes more investment and space, but it'll give your online presentations an elegant feel. It involves the same basic upgrades as your casual arrangement—internet, laptop, mic—plus extra devices used by practiced presenters. For instance, a secondary monitor expands your virtual desktop, allowing you to have more windows open at once. You can position your virtual communication platform app and all of its sub-windows (main meeting room, chat pane, participant pane, participant videos, etc.) on one screen while viewing your speaker notes on another, or you can move things around to your liking. To increase the quality of your video and audio input, get an external webcam and replace your headset or earbuds with a standalone microphone (plug both into your computer).

These audiovisual enhancements are useful for virtual presentations that will be recorded and viewed later on-demand, since audiences often expect higher production values for recorded talks. In a pinch, you can record decent audio and video with a smartphone, but some fidelity is almost always lost in transmission. Starting with high quality on your end will hedge against that risk. Adding extra lighting to your home studio, such as an LED light mounted atop your monitor or standing right behind it, will also elevate the look of your virtual presentation. These peripherals might max out the ports on your computer or electrical outlets, so you may want to include a small USB "hub" device and an extra power strip on your shopping list when buying the other items.

A sophisticated setup demands premium equipment that's fit for an expert speaker or video maker. It starts with a pro-level framework but raises quality with larger and pricier versions of everything, from wall-mounted flat screens to high-end video cameras and photographer-quality lights on tripods. Getting the very best equipment is expensive, but if you have the resources to invest, you'll gain a great deal of flexibility and be ready to handle pretty much any virtual presenting opportunity that comes your way.

To take your gear up another tier, you might spring for a "green screen" if you plan to use slides or images as virtual backgrounds. This special fabric backdrop tricks your camera into treating you and your background as separate objects, because the backdrop is bright neon green and you are not. Green screen kits include the fabric plus a way to suspend it behind you so it will hang smoothly, either clipped to a vertical frame or pinned to a wall. (A small green screen is fine for presentations where you're seated, but if you plan to stand then get one that's taller and wider.) If your virtual communication app has a setting for green screens, click to select it. Now your computer should be able to superimpose video of you on top of other images without making you disappear.

An at-home green screen setup will take some troubleshooting to get a crisp image that appears as realistic as possible. There are a lot of variables to control, including the amount of contrast between you and your background, the positioning of your screen, and the brightness of lights in your room. For instance, if your hair or clothes have greenish tones or if they are too similar to the colors of your virtual background, parts of you will virtually vanish. Try to wear clothes in colors that are the opposite of colors in the virtual image behind you (definitely no green attire), and avoid backgrounds that are too similar to your own coloring (such as a black background against dark hair or a light background against blonde hair). If there's a halo around your face and body, increase the lighting in your room so both you and your green screen are evenly illuminated, because dark spots make it harder for the camera to distinguish you from your backdrop.[71] However, you may still run into snags, especially if your hair is very blonde or gray, as mine is, causing your mane to blend with the light you're aiming at it. If after a few tests your virtual background still gives you trouble, consider switching back to a real background or seek expert advice from an experienced videographer.

For any tech setup, it's a good idea to buy backup devices so you have spares on hand in case one fails. Having doubles is also useful if you sometimes have to travel to present in person; just keep a complete set of peripherals, cables, and dongles packed in a bag that's ready to go. If you're not too resource constrained, consider having two presentation environments in your home or office to accommodate different levels of polish without having to pick up and move your equipment.

Tiffani Bova, the Global Growth and Innovation Evangelist at Salesforce, and author of the best-selling book *Growth IQ*, has a very busy life as a speaker. She typically traveled 200,000 miles or more per year pre-pandemic, delivering keynotes, attending customer meetings, and advising companies around the globe. But when the lockdown curbed her travel, Bova began experimenting with ways to deliver presentations remotely. At first, she simply used her laptop with its built-in webcam and mic, but quickly realized that wasn't going to work long-term. So Bova turned her garage into a professional workspace with three unique areas designed to serve different purposes, such as collaborative meetings, virtual webinars, keynote presentations and videos *(Figure 29)*.

In the first area, Bova has a laptop connected to an external webcam plus two small LED cube lights aimed at a whiteboard where she leads video brainstorming sessions

FIGURE 29

Multi-Purpose Home Studio Used by an Experienced Speaker

A **casual** setup for brainstorms

A **professional** setup for webinars

A **sophisticated** setup for videos

with customers and colleagues. Next to that set up, in the second area, is a standing desk with a separate computer, DSLR camera, ring light, monitor, and microphone, which she uses for recording webinars and podcast interviews. The third area has higher-quality equipment to produce live-streamed video broadcasts, TV interviews, and keynote presentations. It contains another DSLR camera on a tripod, sound-dampening acoustic panels on the ceiling, and three adjustable lights that can be aimed at a green screen or a bookcase to create different backdrop options. While all this equipment is important, the network is the most critical component. In fact, Bova uses two different internet service providers to ensure she can always get a strong connection, along with an uninterruptible power supply device that keeps her equipment running for 30 minutes in the event of a power outage. This array of tech options gives Bova ultimate flexibility for any kind of presentation.

Angle your equipment for best effect

Once you've set up the right equipment and learned how to use it, arrange it to get the benefits you want. This involves making sure the lighting and camera angles are optimal *(Figure 30)*.

To start, aim your lights in the right direction. Your primary lighting should be pointed at your face. When it comes from behind or from odd angles, it casts shadows that can obscure your expressions or make you look ominous. If you've ever been in a virtual meeting with an attendee who had their back facing a window, you probably had a hard time seeing their face because bright light from the sun behind them overexposed the scene. They should have closed their window coverings or moved to a different spot. No tech required to solve that problem; just a change of setting.

For highly-polished virtual presentations, you can try the "three-point lighting" setup used by videographers and photographers:[72] 1) a "key light" (such as a ring LED light) pointed directly at your face, 2) a "fill light" (like your desk lamp) positioned to the side of your face, and 3) a "back light" (another LED light on a tripod or a floor lamp) that's placed farther away but angled toward the back of your head. Together, these three sources of light create an evenly lit scene around you that softens shadows and yields a crisper image.

After adjusting your lighting angles, position your computer and/or camera directly in front of you with the camera at eye level so you can easily look into it when you're speaking.

FIGURE 30

A Sampling of Good and Bad Angles

Bad: backlit scene renders face unreadable

Bad: awkward camera angle, murky lighting

Good: straight-on camera view, proper lighting, gestures visible

Having the camera too far below your face will make you appear to tower over your audience, which can seem arrogant or threatening. Also, if the camera lens is pointing up toward

your face it will give your audience a front-row seat to the sideshow inside your nose. Make sure the lens is straight ahead, even if you need to raise your computer on a stand or a stack of books. Also, as you sort out where you'll sit or stand to frame your face within the screen, remember to keep your hands visible if you plan to use gestures to underscore things you're saying.

While you're futzing with your stuff, take a minute to adjust the mic. It should be a few inches away from your mouth—close enough to capture your voice clearly and at good volume. But don't put it right up to your lips, or the mic will "pop" too loudly when you say explosive consonants like t's and p's.

Display primary information near the lens

One of the biggest delivery challenges for people who are new to virtual presenting is remembering where to look. For a face-to-face presentation, Duarte coaches advise presenters to let their eyes roam around the room to make eye contact with several different audience members rather than locking in on just one person for the duration of their talk. But in an online presentation, we reverse that rule and advise speakers to keep their eyes focused on one place the whole time: the lens of the camera. It might feel strange at first to talk to an inanimate object, but you're not alone. Stage actors who switch to movies also have to warm up to the lens. If they can do it, you can, too.

The camera is the "eye of the audience." Any time you look into that lens, you're talking directly to your viewers, which helps them feel more connected to you. Put whatever you need to see most often during your presentation (your notes, images of participants) at the top-center of your main monitor, near the camera lens, so you can refer to those things without breaking your visual connection with the audience. On your laptop, off to the side, you can display secondary information like your slides and your chat pane within easy glancing distance *(Figure 31)*.

FIGURE 31

Placement of Primary and Secondary Information

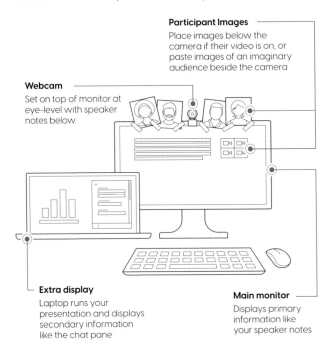

Participant Images
Place images below the camera if their video is on, or paste images of an imaginary audience beside the camera

Webcam
Set on top of monitor at eye-level with speaker notes below

Extra display
Laptop runs your presentation and displays secondary information like the chat pane

Main monitor
Displays primary information like your speaker notes

If you're using speaking notes, it helps to format them for quick scanning. Convert long sentences into short phrases or bullets (5 to 8 words per line), and set them in a large font with wide leading between lines so each word is legible at a glance. When Nancy Duarte records internal video messages for employees, she puts her script into a Word file that she places right below the camera, sort of like a teleprompter. She sets a very narrow column width and scrolls the script continuously while reading it so her eyes don't have to scan the entire width of the screen, making it easier to keep her gaze near the camera the whole time. She also minimizes all toolbars in the application interface so her eyes are less likely to stray while she's talking.

As you look at the camera, keep your audience in view if your participants have their video on. Drag that window near your camera as a visual reminder that you're talking to people, not technology. Scale the window as small as possible to show as many faces as you can. If you are speaking at a webinar with a very large audience and you can't see any faces, try affixing photos of smiling people to the top of your monitor, near the camera. Sometimes I use pictures of crush-worthy celebrities (Paul Rudd has helped me get through several speaking gigs). Those faces will remind you there are humans on the other side of that tiny blue dot, warming your heart when you look into it. Whatever it takes to feel and convey affection for your audience is fair game.

Make the Most of Your Voice

Presentations are, at their core, a spoken-word medium, so one of your most powerful tools is your voice. The best tech in the world can only amplify the signal you naturally put out. Effective vocal delivery brings clarity to your words and vibrancy to your performance. Varying your vocal dynamics will increase your audience's engagement by enhancing emotional appeal, since the voice is second only to the face as a vehicle for expressing feeling.[73]

Speak with precision

Sometimes virtual audiences minimize the speaker's video. When that happens, your voice becomes your main vehicle for your message. While your microphone may pick up audio clearly, the audience's equipment might be lower-fidelity, or their environment could be noisy. To compensate for these challenges, be extra crisp when enunciating so your voice has impact and your words are intelligible at all times. This is especially important if you're addressing people whose primary language or speaking accent is different from yours.

To optimize the process of speaking, it helps to understand how your voice is produced physiologically. When you begin to talk, the air in your lungs is pushed upward by your diaphragm, which acts like a bellows to thrust breath up your windpipe. As the breath passes through your vocal cords, they vibrate rapidly, creating sound waves that are further shaped when channeled into your mouth and nasal passages.[74] Those raw vocalizations are transformed into words as you form, or articulate, various letters with your jaw muscles, tongue, and lips. The more precisely you enunciate each part of each word, the crisper your speech will be and the better your audience will be able to understand you *(Figure 32)*.

Take the following steps to make your voice strong and clear: Start with a strong source—a good dose of oxygen. Sit or stand upright, with your spine relatively straight and your shoulders squared rather than slumping. You want a clear airway. Then begin drawing air in from your belly rather than your chest (you'll know you're doing it right if your stomach puffs out a bit when you inhale). Consciously engage your diaphragm muscles to send your voice out strongly on the exhale. Don't hold your breath—let it ride the exhale. Doing this will increase the strength of your breath so you can project your voice more loudly. Finally, when forming words in your mouth, open your mouth slightly larger than may seem normal in casual speech so the sounds are projected clearly, as if traveling through a megaphone.

FIGURE 32

Conditions for a Strong, Clear Voice

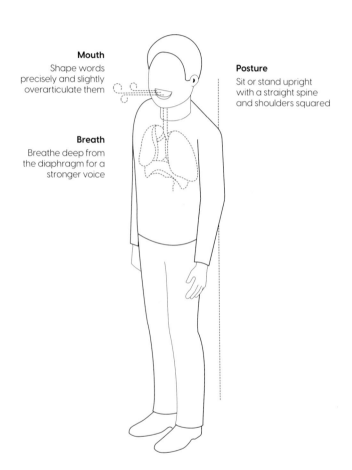

Mouth
Shape words precisely and slightly overarticulate them

Breath
Breathe deep from the diaphragm for a stronger voice

Posture
Sit or stand upright with a straight spine and shoulders squared

As you speak, slightly overarticulate your words to make sure each syllable is distinct. Nicole Lowenbraun, a Duarte executive speaker coach and certified speech pathologist, recommends mouthing words in front of a mirror to practice. If you don't see much movement in your lips or tongue, your words will be mushy or soft, which means audiences may have a hard time understanding you. Just like any other muscle in your body, articulator muscles need a good workout to stay strong. So before an important talk, do some basic warmup exercises like opening your mouth wide, sticking out your tongue, and moving your tongue in big circles.[75]

Vary your voice to add interest

Anytime you adjust something when presenting, including your voice, it'll bring your audience's focus back to you. A monotone voice will cause people to glaze over ("Anyone, anyone? Bueller?")[76] but vocal variety brings life to the virtual room. Grab attention and add emphasis to your words by fluctuating your volume, pace, and pitch *(Figure 33)*.

Like turning a stereo dial, adjusting volume up or down allows you to convey different energy levels. A loud voice makes you seem animated, while a soft voice seems calm, and alternating between the two creates a dynamic feeling. Speeding up or slowing down affects energy, too, though this technique shouldn't be overdone. Speaking too quickly can sound angry or manic, and speaking too slowly can sound as if you're condescending to the audience. You can change the pitch of your voice, going either higher or lower, to signal your intent—raising a question (high pitch), for instance, or making a declaration (low pitch). Much has been written about "uptalk," or upward inflections, a common vocal

FIGURE 33

Techniques for Increasing Vocal Variety

Volume Go louder or softer at key moments	**Pace** Speed up or slow down your tempo	**Pitch** Add up or down inflections to words or phrases
Add punch to a key word by saying it slightly louder Lower your voice to entice listeners to lean in or create suspense	Talk faster to convey urgency Slow down to invite calm Pause briefly before or after an important point	Use higher pitch to seem approachable and inviting, especially when asking more than telling Use lower pitch to seem authoritative and commanding, as when sharing decisions or direction

Emotion
Vary your voice to convey feelings

To convey anger or excitement: speak louder, faster, and higher

To express sadness or gravity: speak softer, slower, and lower

pattern where the speaker's pitch consistently rises at the ends of sentences, though opinions differ on how it helps or hurts persuasive communication.[77] Regardless of personal preferences, everyone has a natural pitch range, and it is directly related to the size and shape of your vocal cords. While you can't easily change your anatomy, you can make some adjustments within your natural range using these techniques.

All three vocal qualities—volume, pace, and pitch—can be combined to reflect the emotional state of the speaker and provide emotional cues to the audience.[78] For example, you can increase pace or volume to generate excitement when explaining a fresh insight or new feature. You can also increase the volume or pitch of your voice, or insert a brief pause, to bring extra "punch" to a point so your audience really feels your conviction. Longer pauses can signal gravity and allow your audience to reflect and absorb what you just said. These quiet moments can be especially beneficial if you're presenting without slides.

When you modulate your voice, variety is the key. Too much of the same thing—same volume, pace, pitch—will lose your audience's attention, so change things up. You can get a boost of variety by sharing the virtual stage with a co-presenter whose vocal style is different from yours.

It may sound like a lot of effort to incorporate all of these vocal techniques into your delivery. But you can acquire the skills gradually. Start by trying one or two techniques at key moments in a talk. As you rehearse with your notes, highlight a couple of important words you really want to bring home. Then practice emphasizing those words—perhaps adjusting the pitch of your voice when saying a catchphrase you want everyone to remember, or slowing down during the final part of a story to "stick the landing."

One of Duarte's clients, a CEO, had a tendency to rush through her scripts for all-hands meetings, especially when talking about major accomplishments. Because she spoke so speedily, statements that should have garnered applause from her employees were instead met with silence, most likely because her audience was simply taking it all in. With the help of a speaker coach, the CEO learned to slow down slightly and add a few strategic pauses to emphasize major points. The result? At her next all-hands meeting, employees applauded the big wins and showed engagement by asking questions throughout. The meeting ran overtime.

Move With Intention

Studies using eye-tracking technology show that the speaker's face is where people look most often during presentations. That's true for both in-person and video-based interactions.[79] So facial expressions—smiles, grimaces, arched brows—are automatically on the audience's radar. The body commands attention, as well. In particular, speakers can underscore their ideas through motion—and they can draw focus to the movements of their head, shoulders, arms, and hands with additional body language. For instance, a speaker might point to their watch when referencing the time or look to the sky when speaking of the weather.

These expressions—"kinesics"[80] —are considered nonverbal because they're not words you say but actions you perform. But the interplay between movement and language can be very powerful. Since virtual presenters are highly visible— audiences can see speakers much more clearly on screen than on stage—you need to be extra cognizant of what your body is doing so you can communicate effectively and make a good impression. If you're using gestures, keep your hands visible within the frame. When you're not making an important point, it's okay to let your hands move out of view and rest on your lap or desk. (Occasionally not using your hands is another form of contrast that adds variety to your presentation.)

Deliberate movements need to be seen because nonverbal expression aids communication. For example, studies have found that when speakers use their hands to indicate the size or location of an object that isn't visible, the audience can better understand its properties.[81] Various studies have confirmed that nonverbal communication aids learning when teachers combine spoken words with gestures to clarify or reinforce what is being taught.[82] Gestures are also an especially empathetic way to support hearing-impaired audiences, so consider hiring an interpreter to sign during your talk.

Various types of nonverbal expression have been identified and studied by psychologists like Paul Ekman and Wallace Friesen, whose research identified five categories of nonverbal behavior: emblems, illustrators, adapters, regulators, and affect displays.[83] These various kinds of movements and expressions are often combined in persuasive communication to intentionally underscore a point that the speaker is making. In particular, you can use nonverbal communication within your virtual presentations to amplify your message, to signify meaning, and to delineate physical qualities *(Figure 34)*.

FIGURE 34

Nonverbal Gestures Useful for Presenting

Amplifiers Motions used to add emphasis	**Signifiers** Motions used to convey concepts	**Delineators** Motions used to specify qualities
Making facial expressions (smiling, grinning, grimacing, frowning) that convey emotions you want people to feel	Using hands to draw an object in the air (heart, circle, box, triangle, etc.)	Widening the eyes or mouth while also describing something very large
Wiggling hands up and down in excitement	Pointing to someone to indicate you are speaking to or about them	Holding hands close together or far apart to indicate a small or large distance between two objects
Lifting outstretched palms in the air to convey joy or elation	Miming an act like putting on a hat	Raising a hand up to show increasing or rising numbers, or moving it down to show decreasing or falling numbers
Clutching hand to heart when expressing love or intense feeling	Forming fingers into shapes with cultural meaning (peace, hang ten, etc.) or numbers (1 to 10)	Tracing the arc of a line on a chart
Moving hands rhythmically in time with speech		

Amplify your message

Amplifiers are motions that add emphasis to our vocalizations so people can more deeply experience what we're feeling. These movements are often automatic. We use them naturally as we speak, often without making a literal connection to the words we choose. Think of a little boy who's just been given a new toy: As he squeals with delight, he flaps his hands up and down like a Muppet on strings. Other motions convey more specific emotions. People often lift their arms in the air to express joy, place a hand over the heart to show love, or applaud when they like something they heard. Some people even move their hands rhythmically in time with the pace of their speech, the way orchestra members tap their feet with the music, creating a physical tempo that matches the sound.

Amplifiers help build a connection with your audience, as well. By capturing and emphasizing your own emotions through physical gestures and facial expressions, you can model the emotions you want others to feel, bringing you closer together. This is a powerful technique for video-only presentations, where people can easily see your expressions. You can even move your hands closer to or farther from the camera to magnify the effect. When Nancy Duarte was communicating with employees throughout the pandemic in 2020, she recorded weekly video memos to keep people up to date on developments and leave them reassured and inspired. In one of the videos *(Figure 35)*, she used her hands in different ways to amplify ideas and emotions, such as putting her hand over her heart when expressing affection and resting her head on her hand during a somber moment. She also formed the ASL sign for "brave," a symbol the company had learned and internally adopted early in the pandemic. As Duarte formed the sign, she moved her hands closer to the camera so employees could see and feel it fully, giving them just the kind of encouragement they needed.

FIGURE 35

Sample Amplifiers Used by a CEO

Signify meaning

Signifiers are motions used as symbols, without any need for words to explain them. An obvious example is when you hold up fingers to represent a number, like two or five or ten. You're also using a symbol when you put your hands together in the shape of a heart to express affection or approval of an idea. Pointing at yourself or someone else can signify who you are talking about. Miming the act of putting an imaginary cap on your head or straightening a tie while telling a story about someone creates a mental image of that person.

Of course, some symbols have ambiguous or fluid meanings, because cultural norms and individual interpretations influence how people read them. Signifiers that seem fine to use in your close circle of friends or colleagues may be off-putting to others. To an American, for instance, a "thumbs-up" wordlessly says that everything is awesome, whereas in other countries it's a rude insult.[84] If you have to give a presentation in a region that's unfamiliar to you, research gestures considered positive or negative in your audience's culture to avoid offending people.

Delineate physical qualities

Delineators are motions that convey spatial information like size, distance, or trajectory so your audience can better understand the properties of an object or data set or grasp the magnitude of an abstract idea. A salesperson might pinch their thumb and forefinger together to show he is "this close" to landing a deal. Or a scientist delivering a report on rising sea levels might lift her hand a certain number of feet above the ground in front of her to indicate what the increase would look like in a way the audience can easily process.

You can also use delineators to interpret your slides so people can follow what you're showing them. For instance, you might trace lines on a graphic with your finger, as you would with a laser pointer, while explaining a model or framework.

Or when you're describing a trend—say, a cost that's rising or a level of investment that's dropping—you might raise or lower your hands as you explain the peaks or valleys on the slide. Nancy Duarte often uses her hands to draw attention to key words on her slides and to delineate what they mean. In one keynote where Duarte explains the use of action verbs as a device for communicating insights from data, she drops her hand low when referencing the verb "create," establishing it as a baseline, then raises her hand when referencing the verb "disrupt", to indicate it is a step above the usual—a more strategic word choice *(Figure 36)*.

FIGURE 36

Sample Delineators Used by a CEO

Drop hand to establish the first phrase as a baseline

Raise hand to convey the second phrase is a step above

Align movement and message

As you're incorporating facial expressions, gestures, and other nonverbal elements, it's essential that they align with what you're saying. Gestures that point or create shapes carry very specific meanings, so they should be used precisely to match your words or graphics. If there's a mismatch, it creates dissonance, which may confuse people or, worse, undermine their trust.

Also, make sure your face and body don't say anything about you that you don't want to convey. For example, if you tend to use overly animated gestures when you're excited or nervous, like rocking back and forth, those might visually overwhelm your audience or cause them to doubt your confidence or competence. Spend some time watching videos of your past presentations to identify which gestures are common for you and whether they are expressing the feelings and projecting the image you want.

If you're trying a movement technique that's new for you, it might feel awkward at first, and you may even worry that you're "bombing" because it's hard to read a remote audience's reaction. Do a practice run in front of a small, friendly test audience so you'll know if you're getting the reaction you want. Working with a speaker coach is another great way to hone your delivery. You'll get pointed feedback to help you polish your presentation style so you're ready for the virtual stage.

Be mindful of your energy

Presenting online takes energy—lots of it. Anyone who does it for a living, like Duarte's training facilitators, will tell you that communicating virtually is far more taxing than presenting in person because they're working so many mental muscles at once. You've got to communicate your key talking points in just the right way with your eyes fixed on the camera. Meanwhile, you're periodically sneaking quick peeks at the chat so you don't miss an urgent message from your producer or an important question from your viewers. It's like being on stage and in the audience at the same time, and that can leave you exhausted at the end.

More than once after giving a big virtual presentation, I felt so tired I wanted to nap (but couldn't because I was booked to attend yet another virtual meeting). I've learned the importance of self-care, before and after the event, to make sure my energy tank starts out full and gets replenished as I go through my day. It comes down to simple things: get a good night's rest, squeeze in a little exercise or stretching, don't skip meals, and stay hydrated. If you tend to have a little anxiety about speaking, do a short mindfulness exercise— like deep breathing—to calm your nerves and regain your center about 30 minutes or so before your talk begins. A lot of speakers have their own preferred rituals when preparing for a talk, so find one that works for you.[85] When you invest in yourself, the audience will feel the difference, and you'll discover, as I have, that the effort pays off in higher engagement and virtual applause in the end.

Move With Intention

Conclusion
Make a World of Difference

Thanks to virtual presentations, the world got a lot smaller. With a simple but high-quality technology setup in your office or home, plus the techniques you learned in this book, you can communicate and connect with audiences anywhere.

Imagine the possibilities that presenting online opens up simply because you can convey your messages to any audience, in any time zone. As your reach increases, so will your influence. Your ideas will fly much faster and farther, making you a more valuable contributor at work, whatever your level or role. And you'll raise your profile as a promising candidate for new assignments and job opportunities. Communication was already one of the chief soft skills employers looked for when recruiting talent.[86] Now that digital technologies are transforming entire companies and sectors—not to mention work itself—remote interactions are becoming more norm than exception. That means we can add virtual presentations to the list of vital soft skills. Whether you're an individual contributor, a team leader, or a senior executive, you'll need to connect with people at a distance to persuade them and move them. From here on out, mastering that capability will be essential to your success.

You might even build a career as a virtual presenter to get your ideas out there, as many leaders in their fields have begun to do. Consider, for example, the rise of TED Talks. Initially, presentations were delivered to a small group of in-person attendees. But when TED launched a new website in 2007, recorded versions of those same presentations were seen by a vast global audience, giving professionals of all kinds a whole new level of exposure.[87] Physicians like Hans Rosling, psychologists like Angela Lee Duckworth, novelists like Chimamanda Adichie, and even introverts like Susan Cain became widely known. Now, more digital platforms are emerging to give virtual presenters a larger audience.

Online training and education platforms like LinkedIn Learning, Degreed, and Udemy allow experts in all domains to share their insights with anyone in the world.

Life has dramatically changed for all presenters, even professional speakers. Many of us breathed a sigh of relief when events suddenly went virtual. At first, it was simply a matter of convenience—not having to hop on a plane to get to our next speaking gig meant feeling less stressed and getting extra rest. But now we're recognizing a more profound benefit: boundless opportunity. One top-tier presenter I know—a management consultant—saw demand for her talks on innovation explode merely because there were more open slots on her calendar. She doubled her bookings and increased her impact just by staying home.

It's easier than ever to get your ideas in front of a massive audience, so be ready to give your best performance when the virtual spotlight shines on you. Wherever you are on the spectrum of virtual presenters, from beginner to pro, you have the tools and the know-how to keep expanding your reach and influence. You have your platform. Now use it to make a difference.

Appendix

Virtual Presentation Checklist

When it's your turn to step into the virtual spotlight, use this checklist as a handy guide to plan, craft, and deliver an engaging online presentation that will keep your audience engrossed.

Strategy

Empathize with your audience

- ☐ Understand who they are, but also how they might think and feel about your idea

- ☐ Consider the environment they'll be in when viewing your presentation and what will make it easy to access and consume

Pick a presentation format

- ☐ Plot where you think the audience stands on your idea, where you want them to stand, and what you will say or do to move them

- ☐ Determine if your presentation should be linear (one-way), interactive (two-way), or collaborative (multi-way), and delivered live or recorded

- ☐ Decide if you will need a co-presenter, moderator, or technical producer to assist you

Think in 3D

- ☐ Consider how you will manage all three layers of information: backdrop, visuals, presenter

- ☐ Think about how those layers will come together to establish the look and tone you want

Story

Craft consumable content

- ☐ Brainstorm ideas for topics to cover, limiting yourself to one-idea-per-slide

- ☐ Group topics into bite-sized "chunks" of information, organized into three sections: beginning, middle, end

- ☐ Get creative with your opening, transition, and closing statements

Incorporate story elements and contrast

- ☐ Build tension and release it by alternating between "what is" and "what could be"

- ☐ Add emotional impact with stories

- ☐ Mix up content types and formats to add variety

Orchestrate purposeful interactions

- ☐ Match interaction types to your goals and your audience's needs: simple, moderate, or complex

- ☐ Decide when interactions will happen and how you will direct the audience to participate

Visuals

Curate your backdrop

- ☐ Choose the level of "polish" for your presentation: casual, professional, or sophisticated

- ☐ Look at your environment as the audience will see it, through the camera lens

- ☐ Remove any clutter or visual distractions and curate remaining items for a pleasing image

Design your graphics

- ☐ Simplify slides by removing excess content and visualizing the most important ideas

- ☐ Accentuate the right elements on each slide to draw your audience in and keep their interest using variety and contrast

Plan your presence

- ☐ Decide if you will sit or stand while speaking

- ☐ Apply the "rule of thirds" to frame where your face and body appear on screen

- ☐ Select attire that complements your graphics and doesn't create visual noise

Delivery

Step up your setup

☐ Ensure your room is sound-friendly by situating yourself in a quiet space, softening ambient sounds, and silencing other apps, devices, or objects

☐ Match your technology to the level of polish needed: consumer, prosumer, or expert

☐ Position your camera at eye-level and aim lights toward your face

☐ Place speaker notes near the camera to avoid looking away from the lens

Make the most of your voice and movement

☐ Vary the volume, pace, and pitch of your voice

☐ Adopt good posture for a strong, clear voice

☐ Maintain eye contact

☐ Move within the frame and use gestures with intention to amplify feelings, signify concepts or objects, or delineate qualities of the things you describe verbally

☐ Manage your energy by practicing self-care and using rituals to prepare before you present and refresh afterward

Glossary

Accessibility
Designing communication so it accommodates all audiences.

Annotations
A feature in virtual meeting platforms and screensharing applications
that allows people to annotate (draw, write, add emojis) on a slide or
other shared image.

Attentiveness/Attention
See Virtual Audience Attention.

Audience
People who are on the receiving end of communication. More specifically,
the viewers of a presentation, whether it is of the linear, interactive, or
collaborative type. See Linear Presentation, see Interactive Presentation,
and see Collaborative Presentation.

Audience Engagement
See Virtual Audience Engagement.

Audiovisual Enhancements
Technological enhancements to help with the delivery of successful audio
and video to audience members within a virtual communication setting.

Brainstorm
A collaborative process used by people to create, explore, and invent.

Breakouts
A feature in virtual meeting platforms and screensharing applications
that allows people to move from one common virtual space to another
virtual sub-space with a selection of participants from the common
space. It is the same as a breakout room at an event, but virtual.

Breakout Rooms
See Breakouts.

Camera
See Webcam.

Chat
A feature in virtual meeting platforms and screensharing applications that allows people to communicate via a stream of text-based communication that is visible in real time.

Chunking
Breaking content into small pieces of information that are designed to be consumed in bite-sized portions.

Collaborative Presentation
Multi-way communication. A speaker and audience members communicate back and forth in collaboration to achieve goals. See Strategy section, *Figure 7, page 47.*

Delivery
The sending of communication to an audience by a speaker; a component of public speaking skills.

Designed Conversation
A discussion or conversation that is designed to move the speaker and audience from point A to point B, while providing opportunities for organic communication within.

Digital Whiteboard
A feature in virtual meeting platforms and screensharing applications, or a stand-alone application, that allows a speaker and/or their audience to write or draw on a shared digital canvas.

Duarte Presentation Sparkline™
A persuasive presentation format that uses tension to help move audiences from the status quo to what could be. Often applied to presentations that use narrative. See Story section, *Figure 13, page 72.*

Glance Test™
A test to be used with presentation slides to know if a viewer can glance at them briefly, glance away from them, and understand what that slide was trying to accomplish.

Green Screen
A physical backdrop made of green fabric that is employed during virtual presentations to allow a speaker to superimpose their video onto a digital background such as slides or images.

Interactions
See Virtual Audience Engagement.

Interactive Tools
See Virtual Audience Engagement.

Interactive Presentation
Two-way communication. A speaker presents to an audience and the audience provides feedback in the form of verbal and nonverbal communication. See Strategy section, *Figure 7, page 47*.

Levels of Virtual Presentation Polish
There are three levels of polish for virtual presentations: casual, professional, and sophisticated. Each level dictates a particular kind of production quality and technology approach for the virtual presentation. See Visuals section, *Figure 20, page 99*.

Linear Presentation
One-way dissemination of ideas. A speaker communicates to an audience without feedback from an audience. See Strategy section, *Figure 7, page 47*.

Microphone (or Mic)
Technology that picks up and transmits sound waves. Microphones are often included within computers and can also be bought and hooked up separately.

Moderator
See Virtual Presentation Moderator.

Nonverbal Gestures
Nonverbal communication cues that amplify your message, signify meaning, and delineate physical qualities. See Delivery section, *Figure 34, page 155*.

Online Virtual Meeting Platforms
See Virtual Meeting Platforms.

Producer
See Virtual Presentation Producer.

Proximity
Distance between speaker and audience, objects, settings, and more.
See Virtual Proximity.

Remote Presentations
See Virtual Presentation.

Slidedoc™
Visual documents developed in presentation software that are intended to be read and referenced instead of projected.

Slides
Presentation aids developed in presentation software that display design and text during a presentation.

S.P.A. Treatment™
Simplifying, planning, and accentuating the right elements on your slides for a virtual presentation to create a pleasing visual experience.
See Visuals section, *Figure 22, page 111.*

Transitions
Words or phrases that bridge one idea with another. Often used to bridge one section with another to help the audience follow along throughout, from beginning to the end.

TriCast Method™
Curating three layers of information in a virtual presentation that are seen within a viewer's screen (the presenter, their backdrop and their graphics).

Video Camera
See Webcam.

Virtual Audience Attention
The degree to which a virtual audience member is giving their attention to the virtual presentation.

Virtual Audience Engagement

Including, and interacting with, a virtual audience using feedback and engagement tools within virtual communication platforms, such as visual and verbal feedback, chat, Q&A, polling, breakouts, whiteboarding, annotation, and more.

Virtual Background

The artificial visual environment around you that is visible to others within a virtual environment. See Virtual Environment.

Virtual Communication Platforms

See Virtual Meeting Platforms.

Virtual Environment

The visual environment around you that is visible to others within a virtual environment. See Virtual Background.

Virtual Filter

An artificial layer (filter) that may be used to alter the appearance of a speaker and their virtual environment to polish, distort, and/or otherwise change what the viewer sees.

Virtual Medium

The virtual channel, or medium, to which one communicates through and within.

Virtual Meeting

A meeting that occurs online, often through a virtual conference platform.

Virtual Meeting Platforms

Applications that allow people to meet virtually from a variety of geo-locations. Can have a variety of features, including but not limited to voice communication, text communication, video communication, and engagement and interaction features.

Virtual Presence

The extent to which one feels the presence of and human connection with others within a virtual medium, such as a virtual meeting platform.

Virtual Presenter

A person, or set of persons, who present or deliver information in a virtual medium.

Virtual Presentation

A presentation that is delivered in a virtual medium, such as through a virtual meeting platform. Virtual presentations can at times be viewed live, and others are viewed as recorded content.

Virtual Presentation Moderator

Someone who facilitates and moderates online communication between the speaker and the audience, and between audience members.

Virtual Presentation Producer

Someone who manages the technical production of a virtual presentation and ensures that the presentation runs smoothly on the virtual platform.

Virtual Proximity

The space between a person and their webcam or objects within their virtual setup. Can also mean the closeness one person feels to another when communicating over a virtual medium, such as a virtual meeting platform. See Proximity.

Vocal Variety

Using a variety of vocal techniques to create a range of ways to deliver your vocal communication, such as: tone, pitch and intonation, volume, pauses, and more or fluctuating your volume, pace, and pitch. See Delivery section, *Figure 32, page 148.*

Webcam

A camera that either comes with a computer or is an add-on device; used by a presenter to capture and send their image via a virtual medium.

Webcast

A live or pre-recorded virtual presentation. See Webinar.

Webinar

A live or pre-recorded virtual presentation. See Webcast.

References

Introduction

1   Mason, Lauren, Kelly O'Rourke, Mary Ann Sardone, Kate Bravery. "The New Shape of Work is Flexibility for All." *Mercer*, 2020. https://www.mercer.com/our-thinking/career/the-new-shape-of-work-is-flexibility-for-all-global.html.

2   Micheli, Valentina. "Benefits of Virtual Events: Why They are Here to Stay." *LinkedIn*, March 27, 2021. https://www.linkedin.com/pulse/benefits-virtual-events-why-here-stay-valentina-micheli/.

3   Lavelle, Justin. "Gartner CFO Survey Reveals 74% Intend to Shift Some Employees to Remote Work Permanently." *Gartner*, April 3, 2020. https://www.gartner.com/en/newsroom/press-releases/2020-04-03-gartner-cfo-surey-reveals-74-percent-of-organizations-to-shift-some-employees-to-remote-work-permanently2.

4   Costello, Katie, Meghan Rimol. "Gartner Says Worldwide End-User Spending on Cloud-Based Web Conferencing Solutions Will Grow Nearly 25% in 2020." *Gartner*, June 2, 2020. https://www.gartner.com/en/newsroom/press-releases/2020-06-02-gartner-says-worldwide-end-user-spending-on-cloud-based-web-conferencing-solutions-will-grow-nearly-25-percent-in-2020.

5   Sawers, Paul. "Virtual Events Came of Age in 2020, But the Future is Hybrid." *VentureBeat*, December 24, 2020. https://venturebeat.com/2020/12/24/virtual-events-came-of-age-in-2020-but-the-future-is-hybrid/.

6   Parker, Kim, Juliana Horowitz, Rachel Minkin. "How the Coronavirus Outbreak Has – and Hasn't – Changed the Way Americans Work." *Pew Research Center*, December 9, 2020. https://www.pewresearch.org/social-trends/wp-content/uploads/sites/3/2020/12/PSDT_12.09.20_covid.work_fullreport.pdf.

Section 1

7   Machemer, Teresa. " 'Zoom Fatigue' May Be with Us for Years. Here's How We'll Cope." *National Geographic*, April 13, 2021. https://www.nationalgeographic.com/science/article/zoom-fatigue-may-be-with-us-for-years-heres-how-well-cope.

8   McLuhan, Marshall, Eric McLuhan. *Laws of Media: The New Science*. Toronto, Canada: University of Toronto Press, 1992.

9   Duarte, Nancy. *HBR Guide to Persuasive Presentations*. MA: Harvard Business Review Press, 2012. https://www.duarte.com/books/hbr-guide-to-persuasive-presentations/.

10 JDP. "Study: Working from Home During the Pandemic." 2020. https://www.jdp.com/blog/work-from-home-statistics/.

11 Poldrack, Russell. "Multi-tasking: The Brain Seeks Novelty." *Huffington Post*, November 17, 2011. https://www.huffpost.com/entry/multitasking-the-brain-se_b_334674#.

12 Cell Press. "Pure Novelty Spurs the Brain." *Science Daily*, August 27, 2006. https://www.sciencedaily.com/releases/2006/08/060826180547.htm.

13 Cigna. "Loneliness and the Workplace: 2020 U.S. Report." January 2020. https://www.cigna.com/static/www-cigna-com/docs/about-us/newsroom/studies-and-reports/combatting-loneliness/cigna-2020-loneliness-report.pdf.

14 Moss, Jennifer. "Dealing with Social Isolation." *SHRM*, April 25, 2020. https://www.shrm.org/hr-today/news/all-things-work/Pages/dealing-with-social-isolation-due-to-coronavirus.aspx.

15 Abbott, Alison. "COVID's Mental-Health Toll: How Scientists are Tracking a Surge in Depression." *Nature*, February 3, 2021. https://www.nature.com/articles/d41586-021-00175-z.

16 Hawthorne, Hayley. "Presenting Virtually: A 2021 Survey Report." *Duarte*, 2021. https://www.duarte.com/resources/virtual-presentations-research-report/.

17   Ibid.

18   Lietz, Jeana. "*Journey to the Neighborhood: An Analysis of Fred Rogers and His Lessons for Educational Leaders*." PhD diss., Layola University Chicago, 2014. https://ecommons.luc.edu/cgi/viewcontent.cgi?article=2096&context=luc_diss.

19   Weiss, Norman. "Stephen Colbert says He Feels More Intimately Connected to His Viewers Doing *A Late Show* Without an Audience." PrimeTimer, December 1, 2020. https://www.primetimer.com/item/-Stephen-Colbert-says-he-feels-more-intimately-connected-to-his-viewers-doing-A-Late-Show-without-an-audience-QwSZdE.

20   Skretvedt, Randy, Christopher H. Sterling. "Radio: Broadcasting." *Encyclopedia Britannica*, 2011, 2018. https://www.britannica.com/topic/radio.

21   Voils, Jessie Wiley. "I'm in New York." *Delineator*, Old Magazine Articles, February 1937. http://www.oldmagazinearticles.com/first_television_broadcast_reaction_article-pdf.

22   Seitz, Matt Zoller. "What TV Owes to Ernie Kovacs." *Salon*, April 18, 2011. https://www.salon.com/2011/04/18/ernie_kovacs_dvd_box_set/.

23   Van Horne, Harriet. "The Chicago Touch." *Rich Samuels*. https://www.richsamuels.com/nbcmm/tct.html.

24   Berkowitz, Joe. "How the 'Tonight Show with Jimmy Fallon' Pivoted During Quarantine and Reinvented Itself." *Fast Company*, April 3, 2020. https://www.fastcompany.com/90483539/how-the-tonight-show-with-jimmy-fallon-pivoted-during-quarantine-and-reinvented-itself.

25   Perez, Leandro. "How to Turn an In-Person Event into a Great Virtual Event." *Salesforce*, March 24, 2020. https://www.salesforce.com/blog/pivot-live-stream-virtual-event-fast-business/.

26   Salesforce. "What Is Dreamforce to You 2020?" November 19, 2020. https://www.salesforce.com/news/stories/what-is-dreamforce-to-you-2020/.

27   Rolfe, Tom. "WWDC 2020 Recap – Everything We Learned This Past Week." *TapSmart*, June 28, 2020. https://www.tapsmart.com/news/wwdc-2020-recap-everything-learned-past-week/.

28   Bejan, Bob. "Digital Transformation of Live Events: Observations from the Front Line." *LinkedIn*, March 13, 2020. https://www.linkedin.com/pulse/digital-transformation-live-events-observations-from-front-bob-bejan/.

Section 2

29   Soeiro, Loren. "Three Things You Need to Know About Perspective-Taking." *Psychology Today*, September 23, 2020. https://www.psychologytoday.com/us/blog/i-hear-you/202009/three-things-you-need-know-about-perspective-taking.

30   3W3C World Wide Web Consortium. "How to Make Your Presentations Accessible to All." *W3C Web Accessibility Initiative*, 2021. https://www.w3.org/WAI/teach-advocate/accessible-presentations/.

31   Hovland, Carl, Muzafer Sherif. *Social Judgment: Assimilation and Contrast Effects in Communication and Attitude Change*. New Haven, CT: Yale University Press, 1980, 1961.

32   Cao, Hancheng, Chia-Jung Lee, Shamsi Iqbal, Mary Czerwinski, Pricilla Wong, Sean Rintel, Brent Hecht, Jaime Teevan, Longqi Yang. "Large Scale Analysis of Multitasking Behavior During Remote Meetings." *Microsoft* (CHI Conference on Human Factors in Computing Systems, May 8-13, 2021). https://dl.acm.org/doi/10.1145/3411764.3445243. https://www.microsoft.com/en-us/research/publication/large-scale-analysis-of-multitasking-behavior-during-remote-meetings/.

33   Durkheim, Émile. *The Elementary Forms of the Religious Life. Translated and with an Introduction by Karen E. Fields*. NY: The Free Press, 1995.

34 Short, John, Ederyn Williams, Bruce Christie. *The Social Psychology of Telecommunications*. NY: Wiley, 1976.

35 Catherine Oh, Jeremy Bailenson, Gregory Welch. "A Systematic Review of Social Presence: Definition, Antecedents, and Implications." *Frontiers in Robotics and AI 5*, no. 114 (2018): 1-35. https://www.frontiersin.org/article/10.3389/frobt.2018.00114.

Section 3

36 Lenz, Peter H., Jennifer McCallister, Andrew Luks, Tao T. Le, Henry Fessler. "Practical Strategies for Effective Lectures." *Annals of the American Thoracic Society* 12, no. 4 (2015): 561-566. https://doi.org/10.1513/AnnalsATS.201501-024AR.

37 Vidyard. "2019 Video in Business Benchmark Report." 2019. https://awesome.vidyard.com/rs/273-EQL-130/images/2019-Video-in-business-benchmark-report_WEB.pdf.

38 Lorenz-Spreen, Philipp, Bjarke Mørch Mønsted, Philipp Hövel, Sune Lehmann. "Accelerating Dynamics of Collective Attention." *Nature Communications* 10, no. 1759 (2019): 1-9. https://doi.org/10.1038/s41467-019-09311-w.

39 Hermitanio, Maui. "'Fear of Missing Out' and Abundance of Information Narrow Global Attention Span, Researchers Say." *Tech Times*, April 22, 2019. https://www.techtimes.com/articles/242023/20190422/fear-of-missing-out-and-abundance-of-information-narrow-global-attention-span-researchers-say.htm.

40 Hawthorne, "Presenting Virtually."

41 Sweller, John, Jeroen van Merriënboer, Fred Paas. "Cognitive Architecture and Instructional Design: 20 Years Later." *Educational Psychology Review* 31 (2019): 261-292. https://doi.org/10.1007/s10648-019-09465-5.

42 Schomaker, Judith. "Unexplored Territory: Beneficial Effects of Novelty on Memory." *Neurobiology of Learning and Memory* 161 (2019): 46-50. https://doi.org/10.1016/j.nlm.2019.03.005.

43   Meznarich, Courtney. "Acts, Scenes, and Sequences – How Long Should Each Be in a Traditional Screenplay?" *SoCreate*, February 26, 2021. https://www.socreate.it/en/blogs/screenwriting/acts-scenes-and-sequences-how-long-should-each-be-in-a-traditional-screenplay.

44   Harrison, Alexa. "4 Tips and 1 Tool That Will Help You Perfect Your Slide Design." *Duarte*. https://www.duarte.com/presentation-skills-resources/perfect-your-slide-design/.

45   Duarte, Nancy. *Resonate: Present Visual Stories that Transform Audiences*. NJ: John Wiley & Sons, Inc, 2010.

46   Duarte, Nancy. "How to Get Others to Adopt Your Recommendation." *Duarte*. https://www.duarte.com/presentation-skills-resources/get-others-adopt-recommendation/.

47   Duarte, Nancy. "How to Move Your Presentation Audience with This Powerful Story Technique." *Duarte*. https://www.duarte.com/presentation-skills-resources/move-presentation-audience-with-story-techniques-in-presentations/.

48   Princeton University. "The Spotlight of Attention is More Like a Strobe." *American Association for the Advancement of Science: EurekAlert!* August 22, 2018. https://www.eurekalert.org/pub_releases/2018-08/pu-tso081718.php.

49   Donley, Melanie, Jeffrey Rosen. "Novelty and Fear Conditioning Induced Gene Expression in High and Low States of Anxiety." *Learning Memory* 24 (2017): 449-461. DOI: 10.1101/lm.044289.116.

50   Morrens, Joachim, Çağatay Aydin, Aliza Janse van Rensburg, José Esquivelzeta Rabell, Sebastian Haesler. "Cue Evoked Dopamine Promotes Conditioned Responding During Learning." *Neuron* 106, no. 1 (2020): 142-153. https://doi.org/10.1016/j.neuron.2020.01.012.

51   Rush, Brianne Carlon. "Science of Storytelling: Why and How to Use It in Your Marketing." *The Guardian*, August 28, 2014. https://www.theguardian.com/media-network/media-network-blog/2014/aug/28/science-storytelling-digital-marketing.

52 Sousa, David. *How the Brain Learns 5th Edition*. CA: Corwin Press, 2017.

53 Parkin, Simon. "Has Dopamine Got Us Hooked on Tech?" *The Guardian*, March 4, 2018, https://www.theguardian.com/technology/2018/mar/04/has-dopamine-got-us-hooked-on-tech-facebook-apps-addiction.

54 Goodman, Andy. "Unmuted: What works, What Doesn't, and How We Can All Do Better When Working Together Online." *The Goodman Center*, 2020, https://www.thegoodmancenter.com/wp-content/uploads/2020/10/Unmuted_GoodmanCenter.pdf.

55 Hawthorne, "Presenting Virtually."

56 Ibid.

Section 4

57 Thomas, Nigel J.T. "Dual Coding and Common Coding Theories of Memory." *Stanford Encyclopedia of Philosophy*, 2014. https://plato.stanford.edu/entries/mental-imagery/theories-memory.html.

58 Paivio, Allan, Kalman Csapo. "Picture Superiority in Free Recall: Imagery or Dual Coding?" *Cognitive Psychology* 5: no. 2 (1973): 176-206. https://doi.org/10.1016/0010-0285(73)90032-7.

59 ANU_V. "Pros and Cons of Visual Learning Style for Students." *Embibe*, April 27, 2021. https://www.embibe.com/exams/visual-learning-benefits-and-strategies-for-students-teachers/.

60 V Renée. "3 Important Elements Production Design Can Bring to Your Film." *No Film School*, June 6, 2018. https://nofilmschool.com/2018/06/3-important-elements-production-design-can-bring-your-film.

61 Jessie, Claude (@RateMySkypeRoom). "Room Rater." *Twitter*. https://twitter.com/ratemyskyperoom.

62 Hawthorne, "Presenting Virtually."

63 Ibid.

64 Duarte. "Simple Presentations: The Glance Test." https://www.duarte.com/simple-presentations-the-glance-test/.

65 Stephens, Maegan. "The Slides You Deliver Versus the Slidedoc You Leave Behind." *Duarte*. https://www.duarte.com/presentation-skills-resources/the-slides-you-deliver-versus-the-slidedoc-you-leave-behind/.

66 Canny, Chariti. "Cut Through the Noise: How to Design Slides for Virtual Presentations." *Duarte*. https://www.duarte.com/presentation-skills-resources/design-slides-for-virtual-presentations/.

67 Michael Bungay Stanier, 2021. https://www.mbs.works.

68 Tabora, Vincent. "The Art of Scale & Framing in Cinema." *Medium*, August 26, 2019. https://medium.com/hd-pro/the-art-of-scale-framing-in-cinema-b9d1109a47a.

69 Framer. "Effective Use of the Rule of Thirds in Design." 2021. https://www.framer.com/dictionary/rule-of-thirds/.

Section 5

70 Koncius, Jura. "Tiny Cloffices – Workspaces in Closets – are Big, Thanks to the Pandemic." *The Washington Post*, May 27, 2021. https://www.washingtonpost.com/lifestyle/home/cloffice-ideas-home-office-closet/2021/05/25/2cb652f2-8d9e-11eb-a6bd-0eb91c03305a_story.html.

71 Simon, Justin. "How to Create a DIY Green Screen Video Effect." *TechSmith*, 2012, 2021. https://www.techsmith.com/blog/how-to-create-a-diy-green-scre/.

72 Karr, Douglass. "How to Set Up 3-Point Lighting for Your Live Videos." *Martech Zone*, October 18, 2020. https://martech.zone/how-to-setup-3-point-lighting/.

73 Hall, Judith A., Terrence G. Horgan, Nora A. Murphy. "Nonverbal Communication," *Annual Review of Psychology* 70 (2019): 271-294. https://doi.org/10.1146/annurev-psych-010418-103145.

74 The Voice Foundation. "Understanding How Voice is Produced." 2021. https://voicefoundation.org/health-science/voice-disorders/anatomy-physiology-of-voice-production/understanding-voice-production/.

75 Baer, Drake. "How the Best Public Speakers Warm Up Their Voices." *Business Insider*, July 3, 2014. https://www.businessinsider.com/how-the-best-public-speakers-warm-up-their-voices-2014-7.

76 Hughes, John, director. 1996. *Ferris Bueller's Day Off*. Paramount Pictures.

77 Kaplan, Abby. " 'Uptalk' in English: Myth and Fact." *Cambridge University Press; World of Better Learning*, January 27, 2017. https://www.cambridge.org/elt/blog/2017/01/27/uptalk-english-myth-fact/.

78 Yanushevskaya, Irena, Christer Gobl, Ailbhe Ní Chasaide. "Voice Quality in Affect Cueing: Does Loudness Matter?" *Frontiers in Psychology* 4, no. 335 (2013): 1-14. https://doi.org/10.3389/fpsyg.2013.00335.

79 Gullberg, Marianne. "Chapter 32: Eye Movements and Gestures in Human Face-to-face Interaction." *In The Mind's Eye: Cognitive and Applied Aspects of Eye Movement Research*, edited by Jukka Hyönä, Ralph Radach, Heiner Deubel, 685-703. North Holland: Elsevier, 2003.

80 Padula, Alessandra. "Kinesics." In *Encyclopedia of Communication Theory*, edited by Stephen Littlejohn, Karen Foss. CA: SAGE Publications, 2009. http://dx.doi.org/10.4135/9781412959384.

81 Beattie, Geoffrey, Heather Shovelton. "Mapping the Range of Information Contained in the Iconic Hand Gestures that Accompany Spontaneous Speech." *Journal of Language and Social Psychology* 18, no. 4 (1999): 438-462. https://doi.org/10.1177/0261927X99018004005.

82   Goldin-Meadow, Susan, Martha Wagner Alibali. "Gesture's Role in Speaking, Learning, and Creating Language." *Annual Review of Psychology* 64, (2013): 257-283. https://doi.org/10.1146/annurev-psych-113011-143802.

83   Ekman, Paul, Wallace V. Friesen. "The Repertoire of Nonverbal Behavior: Categories, Origins, Usage, and Coding." *Semiotica* 1 (1969): 49-98. https://doi.org/10.1515/semi.1969.1.1.49.

84   Cotton, Gayle. "Gestures to Avoid in Cross-Cultural Business: In Other Words, 'Keep Your Fingers to Yourself." *Huffington Post*, August 13, 2013. https://www.huffpost.com/entry/cross-cultural-gestures_b_3437653.

85   Duarte, Nancy. "How to Pump Yourself Up Before a Presentation (or Calm Yourself Down)." *Duarte*. https://www.duarte.com/presentation-skills-resources/how-to-pump-yourself-up-before-a-presentation-or-calm-yourself-down/.

Conclusion

86   McKinsey. "Five Fifty: Soft Skills for a Hard World." *McKinsey Quarterly*, 2021. https://www.mckinsey.com/featured-insights/future-of-work/five-fifty-soft-skills-for-a-hard-world.

87   TED. "History of TED." https://www.ted.com/about/our-organization/history-of-ted.

Photo Credits

Section 1
Figure 1, page 12
Duarte, Nancy. *HBR Guide to Persuasive Presentations*. MA: Harvard Business Review Press, 2012. https://www.duarte.com/books/hbr-guide-to-persuasive-presentations/.

Figure 3, page 31
Salesforce APAC (@salesforceapac). "A big thank you to everyone who tuned in…" *Twitter*, March 3, 2020. https://twitter.com/salesforceapac/status/1235008206432120837/photo/2.

CNET Highlights (@CNETHighlights). "Microsoft CEO keynote for Build 2020." *YouTube*, May 19, 2020. https://www.youtube.com/watch?v=nt_Uy59cK3k.

Apple. "Keynote." *WWDC*, 101, 2020. https://developer.apple.com/videos/play/wwdc2020/101.

Section 2
Figure 6, page 45
Hovland, Carl, Muzafer Sherif. *Social Judgment: Assimilation and Contrast Effects in Communication and Attitude Change*. New Haven, CT: Yale University Press, 1980, 1961.

Figure 13, page 72
Duarte Presentation Sparkline™, Duarte, Nancy. *Resonate: Present Visual Stories that Transform Audiences*. NJ: John Wiley & Sons, Inc, 2010.

Section 4
Figure 24, page 115
Photo courtesy of Michael Bungay Stanier, 2021. https://www.mbs.works

Section 5
Figure 29, page 140
Photo courtesy of Tiffani Bova. 2021. https://www.tiffanibova.com

Duarte graphics designed by: Aisling Doyle, Diandra Macias, Lacey Taylor, Ryan Muta, Chariti Canny, Rico Larroque, Juanly Cabrera, and Shane Tango.

Acknowledgements

I've been delivering presentations online since the Internet was born, but the events of 2020 catapulted me (and everyone I know) into a whole new era of virtual communication. It wasn't totally unfamiliar; most of my clients and many of my colleagues were in other regions, so I already had plenty of practice communicating and connecting with people at a distance. Yet once the pandemic shutdown began, presenting virtually wasn't just one of the things I had to do in a typical day—it was the *only* thing. That meant I not only had to adapt my own approach to communication; I also had to evolve the way my team worked and how we served our customers, too. More specifically, I had to figure out how to flip our Academy's training workshops from fully in-person to fully virtual, transforming our hands-on face-to-face instruction into an immersive, interactive online experience. So, I turned to the experts... my colleagues at Duarte.

When I challenged them to invent a unique take on the virtual workshop format, our writers, designers, facilitators, and producers dove in with gusto—researching customer needs, reimagining workshop agendas, and testing technology platforms to discover how we could push them to their limits. Meanwhile, on the Agency side of Duarte's business, our creative and client services teams were working with some of the world's biggest brands to translate their onsite spectacles into online extravaganzas using innovative presentations that redefined the medium. Inside this book, you'll find our combined wisdom from those pivots.

Everything you read here was sparked by conversations and collaborations I've enjoyed with my many brilliant colleagues at Duarte, affectionately known as "Duartians." These people not only taught me what they know, but also made me a smarter and braver human being.

I'd especially like to thank the following individuals who contributed insights or research on various aspects of online presentations, virtual communication, and distance learning: Catrinel Bartolomeu, Becky Bausman, Chariti Canny, Erik Chappins, Jeff Davenport, Dave DeFranco, Kate Devlin, Cody Dishman, Michael Duarte, Dan Durller, Kevin Friesen, Hayley Hawthorne, Reg Hill, Amanda Holt, Nicole Lowenbraun, Doug Neff, Mike Pastor, Brittany Postler, Mary-Anne Reyes, DJ Rice, Maegan Stephens, Felipa Rodriguez-Stone, and Bryan Thompson. I'd also like to thank Diandra Macias, Aisling Doyle, and many other talented designers at Duarte for their stunning book design; Lisa Burrell for her insightful editing and Emily Williams for her impeccable proofreading; Lacey Taylor, Julie Leong, and Anaykh Tijerina for their masterful project coordination and cat herding skills.

Finally, I want to thank Nancy Duarte for boldly and selflessly deciding to publish this book under the Duarte Press imprint so it could bear my name, not hers. Fearless is the warrior who fights so others can be free. May this book embolden you, dear reader, to lean into your destiny, as it has done for me.

Index

A

Acceptance, 45
Accessibility, 32
  tools, 23, 43
Adapters, 154
Affect displays, 154
Amplifiers, **155**, 156–157
Animated gestures, 160.
     see also Physical gestures;
     Nonverbal gestures
Annotations, 48, 91, 113
  visual, 87
Apple, 32–33
Audience, educating, 67
Audience engagement, 16–17, 25,
    49, 81–83
  case study, 30, 32–34
  communicating instructions,
    90–92
  connecting through cameras,
    27–28
  holding attention with dynamic
    audio, 26
  inventiveness, 28–29
  matching interaction tools with
    situation, 84–85, 87
  sharing direct links, 90–92
  varying levels of interaction,
    88, 90
Audience engagement tools,
    48, 49
  and their uses in virtual
    presentations, 86
Audience participation. *see*
    Audience engagement
Audience's attention
  grabbing, 80–81
  holding, 49, 81–83

Audience size, 47
Audio, dynamic, 26
Audiovisual enhancements, 137
Auditory distractions, 129–130
Augmented reality graphics, 102
Azure cloud computing, 33

B

Backdrop layer, 56, 169
  learning the art of
    scene-setting, 96–98
  matching the environment to
    the moment, 98, 100–102
Bejan, Bob, 33–34
Benefits of virtual presentations
  broader information sharing,
    19–21
  delivering a cohesive
    experience, 23–24
  proximity with the audience,
    21–23
Bova, Tiffani, 139–140
Brainstorm, 39, 47, 69, 70, 139
Breakout rooms. *see* Breakouts
Breakouts, 5, 18, 48, 50, 86, 87,
    90, 92
Built-in noise-cancelling features,
    130
Business casual outfit, 120–123

C

Camera. *see* Webcam
Casual virtual presentation,
    98, 99, 100
Challenges in virtual
    presentations
    distractions, 16–17
    equipment quality, 14–16

isolation, 17–18
Chat, text-based, 49, 53, 87
Choosing format
    assessing audience's stand,
        44–45
    how to interact decisions,
        45–46, 49–50
Chunking in a virtual
    presentation, 66, 67, 69
Clothes for presentation,
    120–123, 138
Cohesive experiences, 23–24
Colbert, Stephen, 22
Collaboration applications, 50, 90
Collaborative presentations,
    47–48, 49–50, 75–76, 77
Collective effervescence, 52
Comfortable speaker, 127
Communication formats and
    content types, 81, 82, 83
Communication in multiple
    dimensions
    bringing all visuals into
    harmony, 54–57
    enhancing virtual presence,
    51–54
Communication platforms,
    43, 104, 108, 109, 131, 136
Complex interactions, 86, 87
Computer for presentation,
    134, 135, 136–138
Consumer-quality equipment,
    134, 135
Content, 61
    chunking information, 64, 66
    curtailing length, 63
    maintaining pace, 64–65, 67, 69
    streamlining argument, 69–70
    structure of a presentation, 68
    types and communication
    formats, 81, 82, 83

Cook, Tim, 33

D
Decision-makers, 40
Degreed, 166
Delineators, 155, 158–159
Designed conversation, 76
Designing graphics
    clarity and contrast,
        109–110, 112–115
    visual hierarchy, 104, 108–109
Digital camera, 136
Digital tools, 4–5
Digital whiteboard, 23, 48, 86, 87
Distractibility, managing
    finishing on a strong note, 83
    grabbing attention in
        first phase, 80–81
    holding attention with variety,
    81–83
Distractions while viewing
    presentations, 42, 43
Dopamine, 17, 81
Dreamforce, 32
Dressing for presentation,
    120–123, 138
DSLR camera, 140
Dual coding, 95
Duarte, Nancy, 11–12, 145, 156, 159
Duarte Presentation Sparkline™,
    71, 73
Dynamic speaker, 127

E
Education platforms, 166
Ekman, Paul, 154
Email, 53, 131
Emblems, 154
Emotions in voice, 150
Empathetic speaker, 127
Empathizing with audience

adopting perspectives, 38–41
viewing environment, 41, 43
End of a presentation, 83
Environmental interference, 81
Ethernet cable, 134
Eye contact, 21, 41, 53, 143–144

F

Face-to-face presentation, 102, 143
Facial expressions, 22, 28, 52, 56, 57, 153, 156
Fallon, Jimmy, 28
Feedback, gathering, 45–46, 160
Friesen, Wallace, 154

G

Garroway, Dave, 28
Gartner, 3
Gestures. *see* Physical gestures
Glance test, 110
Graphics layer, 56
Green screen for presentation, 135–136, 137–138
Growth IQ (Bova), 139

H

HBR Guide to Persuasive Presentations (Duarte), 11–12
Hearing-impaired audiences, 154

I

Illustrators, 154
Informal communication, 100
Information consumption, 43
Instant messaging, 4, 131
Interactions during virtual presentation. *see* Audience engagement
Interactive presentation, 47–48, 49

Internet for presentation, 134, 135, 136–138

J

JDP, 16

K

Kinesics, 153–154
Kovacs, Ernie, 27

L

Laws of Media (McLuhan), 11
Lighting for presentation, 134, 135, 136
Linear presentation, 46, 47–48, 49, 74
LinkedIn Learning, 166
Lowenbraun, Nicole, 148–149

M

McLuhan, Marshall, 11–12
Microphone for presentation, 134, 135, 136–138
Microsoft, 33–34
Mindfulness exercise, 161
Mister Rogers' Neighborhood, 21
Moderate interactions, 86, 87
Moderator, 46, 48, 49, 77, 92
Movements as nonverbal expressions, 153–154

N

Navigational cues, providing, 78–79
Non-Commitment, 45
Nonverbal communication, 53
Nonverbal expressions, movements as, 153–154
Nonverbal gestures, 155. *see also* Physical gestures

aligning movement and
    message, 160
amplifiers, 155, 156–157
deliberate movements, 154
delineators, 155, 158–159
nonverbal behavior, 154
signifiers, 155, 157–158
using energy mindfully, 161
Nonverbal interactions, 52

P

Pace, speaker's, 150, 151
Paivio, Allan, 95
Pauses, 151
Perspective-taking, 38
Persuasive communication,
    44–45, 154
Persuasive structure, 71, 73
Pew Research Center, 4
Photographer-quality lights, 137
Physical gestures, 28, 52, 56, 154.
    see also Nonverbal gestures
Pitch, speaker's, 150, 151
Podcast interviews, 140
Presentation format, 47
Presentation structure, fine-tuning
    going with the flow, 75–76, 78
    providing navigational cues,
      78–79
    story structure, 71, 73, 75
Presenter layer, 56–57
Presenters/speakers
    core traits, 127
    pace, pitch, and volume of,
      150, 151
Pre-workshop email, 90–91
Primacy-recency effect, 83
Producer, 46, 48, 50, 92
Professional virtual presentation,
    99, 100–101
Prompts, 76, 77, 78

Prosumer-quality equipment,
    135, 136–137
Proximity. *see* Virtual proximity

Q

Q&A, 49, 76, 87, 91, 92
Quality products, use of, 14–16

R

R.C.A., 27
Regulators, 154
Rejection, 45
Remote communication, benefits
    of, 19–21
Rogers, Fred, 21
@RateMySkypeRoom, 100

S

Salesforce, 30, 32
Scene-setting, 96–98
Second monitor, 135–136
Signifiers, 155, 157–158
Simple interactions, 85, 86, 87
Slidedoc™, 112
SMS-based polls, 90
Social judgement theory, 45
Social presence, 52–53
Sophisticated setup, 135, 137–138
Sophisticated virtual presentation,
    99, 101–102
Sound-dampening acoustic
    panels, 140
Sound-friendly room, creating,
    129
Space setup
    silencing predictable sounds,
      131–132
    situating in a quiet space,
      128–130
    softening ambient sounds,
      130–131

"S.P.A. Treatment™", 110, 111
Speaker goals, 86
Speaking notes, 145
Steve Jobs Theater, 33
Story prompts, 76, 77, 78
Story structure, 71, 73, 75
Summary technique, 73

T
Tech leaders and virtual events,
        30, 32–34
Technical constraints,
        overcoming, 16–17
Technical producer. see Producer
Technology, optimizing
    displaying primary information
    near the lens, 143-145
    setting equipment for best
    effect, 141–143
    suitable presentation
    technology, 133–134, 136–140
TED Talks, 165
Telepresence, 53
Tension, using, 72
Three-act structure in
        storytelling, 65
"Three-point lighting" setup, 141
Time duration of presentation, 48
Toolbars, minimizing, 145
TriCast Method™, 54, 55
Tripods, 137

U
Udemy, 166

V
Verbal communication, 53
Verbal transitions, 78–79
Video brainstorming sessions,
        139–140

Video cameras, 137.
        see also Webcam
Videoconferencing, 52–53
Video memos, 156
Video messages/ messaging,
        4, 145
Virtual platforms
    skills for, 5–6
    tools in, 4–5
    understanding, 11–13
Virtual presence, enhancing,
        51–54
Virtual presence, planning
    composing the shot, 117,
    119–120
    dressing for the occasion,
    120–123
    posture, 116–117
Virtual presentation polish,
        levels of, 99
Virtual proximity, 21–23
Virtual talk, demerits of, 12
Virtual training workshops, 90–91
Visual aids, 48, 49–50, 92
Visual annotation tools, 87
Visual cues, 78
Visual noise, 123
Visual reminders in webinars, 145
Vocal delivery
    speaking with precision, 146–149
    voice modulation, 149–152
Vocal variety, techniques for, 149,
        150, 151–152
Voice
    conditions for strong and clear,
    148
    varying, 149–152
Volume, speaker's, 150, 151

W

Web-based collaboration
  applications, 50
Webcam, 135, 136
  angles, 141–143
  connection through, 27–28
  proximity, 22
Webcast, 47, 91
Webinars, 47, 91, 140, 145
"White noise" machine, 131
Words, clarity of, 26, 56, 146, 148,
  149
Working memory, 63
Workshop, 47
Worldwide Developer Conference
    (WWDC), 32–33

About the Author

Communication expert Patti Sanchez has more than 30 years of experience leading transformative marketing initiatives for brands and causes. She is co-author of an award-winning book on change communication called *Illuminate: Ignite Change Through Speeches, Stories, Ceremonies, and Symbols*, and her writing has been published in *Fast Company, Forbes, HBR.org*, and *MIT Sloan Management Review*. As Chief Strategy Officer for Duarte, Inc., Sanchez develops product strategies for the training business and teaches executives and teams how to create authentic connections with audiences and to lead change through persuasive communication. She lives in Northern California with her husband, James; their rescue dog, Monty; and a roller canary named Harry Nilsson (aka Harry Canary).

Change Hearts and Minds

Since 1988, Duarte has helped people and organizations worldwide **communicate with greater impact and influence**. We're specialists in the spoken word—the most powerful medium for moving people to believe something new—and we can help you master it, too.

We've codified everything we know into training to teach you, your team, or your entire company to become stronger communicators using the Duarte Method.™ We'll show you how to plan communication with your listeners in mind, shape your ideas into a cohesive story and amplify them with purposeful visuals, and adapt your delivery to better connect with audiences—**all with empathy at the core.**

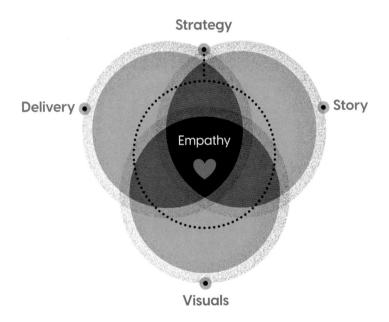

DUARTE

Become a Virtual Presentation Pro

You've got the platform—now practice using it to get your ideas across to remote audiences. Duarte's new Presenting Virtually online course will help you apply techniques in this book to hone your virtual communication. Through short and engaging video-based lessons plus hands-on exercises and reference tools, you'll learn to:

- Choose the right format for your presentation and plan audience interactions
- Chunk your content into consumable bites and organize it into a compelling structure
- Amplify ideas with clear visuals and curate your environment and appearance to match
- Prep your tech and polish your delivery to captivate and connect with your audience

Engaging
video
modules

Presentation
planning tools

Stey-by-step
guidance

65%

Insights from
presentation
experts

Demos of
best practices

Go to duarte.com/presentingvirtually